OFFICIAL GUIDE
TO THE

# NATIONAL AIR

AND

# SPACE MUSEUM

*The Wright brothers changed the world when, on December 17, 1903, at Kitty Hawk, North Carolina, Orville Wright went up in their Flyer for the first successful manned, powered, and controlled flight in a heavier-than-air craft. (NASM photo)*

# OFFICIAL GUIDE
## TO THE

# NATIONAL AIR
### AND
# SPACE MUSEUM

Published for the National Air and Space Museum

by the
**Smithsonian Institution Press**
Washington, D.C.

**Library of Congress Cataloging-in-Publication Data**

National Air and Space Museum.
  Guidebook to the National Air and Space Museum.

  1. National Air and Space Museum—Guide-books.
I. Title
TL506.U6W376  1991          629.13′0074′053
87-600336
ISBN 0-87474-679-5

First edition 1988;
revised 1991, 1993

Printed in Singapore not at government expense

9   8   7   6   5   4   3
99   98   97   96

**Guidebook Staff**
Patricia Jamison Graboske,  *Project Coordinator*
Victoria Jennings Ross, *Writer*
Helen Morrill, *Editor, 1993 Edition*
**Book Development Division Staff, Smithsonian Institution Press**
Caroline Newman, *Executive Editor*
Paula Dailey, *Senior Picture Editor*
Heidi M. Lumberg, *Editor*

We would like to thank the entire staff of the National Air and Space Museum for providing invaluable assistance in preparing this guidebook. In addition, thanks to Tom D. Crouch for reviewing the manuscript, to the staff at VIARC for their helpful suggestions, and to Dane Penland for providing many excellent photographs. We are particularly grateful to Donald S. Lopez for his advice and support during all stages of the project.

*Cover photo: The National Air and Space Museum's Space Hall, as seen from the floor of the missile pit. (NASM photo: C. Russo)*

# CONTENTS

# WELCOME TO THE NATIONAL AIR AND SPACE MUSEUM

Welcome to the National Air and Space Museum. More than 175 million people have come to the Museum since it opened on July 1, 1976. Our visitors come from every state in the Union, and one out of every five comes from abroad.

The Museum is here to bring you a first-hand impression of how aviation and space flight have changed the ways in which we travel by air, prepare for national defense, study the Earth and its resources, and explore the solar system and the universe beyond. This guidebook is designed to call your attention to significant items in the various galleries, and to remind you of highlights of your visit when recalling it to others.

The exhibitions range from a vivid recounting of the beginnings of flight (Early Flight—gallery 107) to the latest techniques of remote sensing (Looking at Earth—gallery 110) and aerospace applications of the digital computer (Beyond the Limits—gallery 213). The 1987 Intermediate Range Nuclear Forces (INF) Treaty between the United States and the Soviet Union, the first step in negotiated nuclear disarmament, is commemorated by a Soviet SS-20 missile standing side by side with an American Pershing II missile in the central Milestones gallery. In our Langley Theater, a new IMAX giant-screen film, entitled *Blue Planet*, shows breathtaking views of Earth seen from space, and describes the natural and manmade forces changing our environment today. In our Einstein Planetarium we portray both historical developments and current discoveries in astronomy. The Museum continues to grow and change in order to reflect new developments in aerospace technology and its applications.

What you see in the Museum's galleries is the product of a highly dedicated staff—including curators and historians, scientists, exhibition designers and producers, airplane and spacecraft restoration specialists, all aided by an enthusiastic army of knowledgeable volunteers. Many of the artifacts you see on display were given by generous donors. Most of the exhibitions were made possible through the financial support of individuals and industry. The annual operating budget we receive from the United States Congress permits us to welcome all of our visitors free of charge.

We hope you and your family will visit the National Air and Space Museum often to enjoy our exhibitions, films, and collections. And if you tell your friends about us, we will be pleased to welcome them as well.

Donald D. Engen
Director
National Air and Space Museum

# NATIONAL AIR AND SPACE MUSEUM

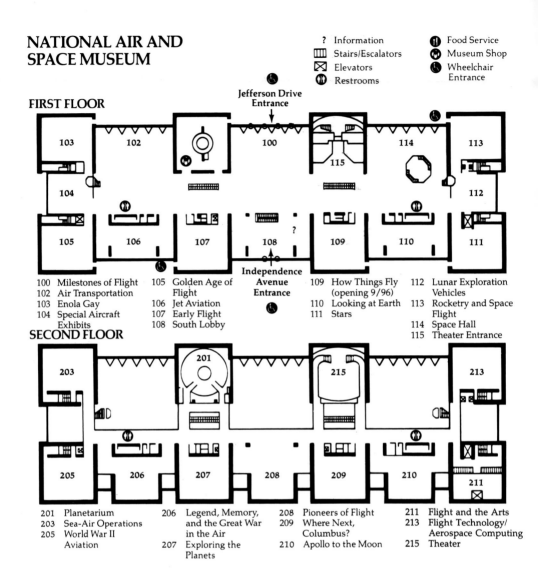

## FIRST FLOOR

Jefferson Drive Entrance

Independence Avenue Entrance

100 Milestones of Flight
102 Air Transportation
103 Enola Gay
104 Special Aircraft Exhibits
105 Golden Age of Flight
106 Jet Aviation
107 Early Flight
108 South Lobby
109 How Things Fly (opening 9/96)
110 Looking at Earth
111 Stars
112 Lunar Exploration Vehicles
113 Rocketry and Space Flight
114 Space Hall
115 Theater Entrance

## SECOND FLOOR

201 Planetarium
203 Sea-Air Operations
205 World War II Aviation
206 Legend, Memory, and the Great War in the Air
207 Exploring the Planets
208 Pioneers of Flight
209 Where Next, Columbus?
210 Apollo to the Moon
211 Flight and the Arts
213 Flight Technology/ Aerospace Computing
215 Theater

# INTRODUCTION TO THE MUSEUM

A visit to the National Air and Space Museum reminds us how far mankind has come in the areas of flight technology and space exploration. Our trip takes us from the sands of Kitty Hawk, North Carolina, to the dusty craters of the Moon's Sea of Tranquillity. It takes us from calendars based on the stars before written history to a life-sized model of the Hubble Space Telescope. We continue to expand our horizons, recognizing that the milestones of science and moments of history represented here are just the beginning.

To tell the story of flight and aerospace technology, the Museum offers 23 galleries, each devoted to a single subject or theme. Visitors are surrounded by visual excitement—theaters, large and small; slide shows; dioramas and diagrams; and a myriad of other innovative devices that invite public participation. Suspended overhead and all around are aircraft, rockets, and spacecraft that have earned their places in history.

The Museum's collection consists of hundreds of historical or technically significant aircraft and spacecraft, along with missiles, rockets, aero engines, propellers, flight equipment, and flight memorabilia. All of the aircraft and most of the manned spacecraft on display here were actually flown. A range of backup vehicles and replicas are exhibited for spacecraft that were not returned to Earth. Only a portion of the collection is exhibited at any one time; some artifacts are held in storage for restoration at the Paul E. Garber Preservation, Restoration, and Storage Facility in Suitland, Maryland. A significant number are on loan to other museums. The Viking Lander, still on Mars, is the Museum's farthest outpost.

The National Air and Space Museum is one of the 16 museums of the Smithsonian Institution. In the early 19th century, the Englishman James Smithson willed his entire fortune to the United States "to found at Washington, under the name of the Smithsonian Institution, an Establishment for the increase and diffusion of knowledge among men." In maintaining exhibits and offering research facilities to the public, the National Air and Space Museum remains true to Smithson's founding mandate.

We hope you enjoy your visit and will return to see our exhibits again soon.

*Twenty-five-year-old Charles Lindbergh made the first solo, nonstop, transatlantic flight in the* Spirit of St. Louis *on May 20-21, 1927. The flight took 33$\frac{1}{2}$ hours. (SI no. 79-763)*

# THE EXHIBITIONS

**Milestones of Flight (Gallery 100)**
Here are the objects that made the dream of flight a reality. Each is a reminder of a noteworthy achievement, and evokes the spirit of its own particular time.

The **Wright 1903 Flyer** is the focal point of the Milestones gallery. On December 17, 1903, the Wright brothers changed the world when Orville went up in this aircraft for the first successful controlled, powered, heavier-than-air flight. Although fragile, the Wright Flyer, which is composed of wood and fabric, and braced with steel wire, achieves a balance between lightness and strength. The Wright brothers constructed the aircraft at their bicycle shop in Dayton, Ohio, and sent it by rail to the coastal dunes of Kitty Hawk, North Carolina, for its flight trials. Museum craftsmen restored the Wright Flyer in a gallery here in 1985, as the public looked on.

In 1896, the **Langley Aerodrome Model No. 5** had demonstrated the possibility of mechanical flight. Designed by Samuel Pierpont Langley, the third Secretary of the Smithsonian Institution, the model was powered by a small steam engine.

This unmanned model made the first significant flight of any engine-driven heavier-than-air craft. It flew twice on the afternoon of May 6, 1896, launched from a houseboat on the Potomac River. Professor Langley's later attempts at manned flight in full-size versions of the Aerodrome were unsuccessful. Also launched from a houseboat anchored in the Potomac, the larger craft hit the water almost immediately after launch in October 1903. A second attempt in early December ended similarly, and

Langley was forced to abandon his dream.

The **Ryan NYP "Spirit of St. Louis"** is one of the most popular objects in all the Smithsonian museums. It is a touchstone of history that is perhaps matched only by the Wright Flyer and the Apollo 11 spacecraft. The *Spirit of St. Louis* was built by the Ryan Company of San Diego, California, for 25-year-old airmail pilot Charles Lindbergh. He took off from Roosevelt Field, Long Island, early on the morning of May 20, 1927, in an attempt to fly solo across the North Atlantic. To see forward, Lindbergh had either to turn the airplane or use a periscope; a gasoline tank was installed where the windshield normally would have been. After $33\frac{1}{2}$ hours, Lindbergh landed at Le Bourget Field, near Paris, welcomed by the frenzied cheers of 100,000 people. He had flown the Atlantic alone, the first solo crossing of a major ocean by air.

Yet another milestone was achieved a little more than 20 years later, when Captain Charles Yeager, U.S. Air Force, flew the bullet-shaped **Bell X-1 "Glamorous Glennis"** (named after his wife, Glennis) faster than the speed of sound. Yeager's rocket-powered flight on October 14, 1947, opened a new era in which research aircraft would lead the way toward spaceflight.

The **Pershing II** and **SS-20** missiles exhibited in the Milestones of Flight gallery are two of more than 2600 nuclear missiles eliminated by the Intermediate-range Nuclear Forces (INF) Treaty, signed by the United States and the Soviet Union in December 1987. These two missiles stand side by side as sym-

*Captain Charles "Chuck" Yeager was the first person to achieve supersonic flight in the Bell X-1* Glamorous Glennis *on October 14, 1947. (SI no. 79-756)*

*The SS-20 and Pershing II missiles stand side by side as symbols of human, rather than technological, achievement— the first international agreement to ban an entire class of nuclear missiles. (NASM photo)*

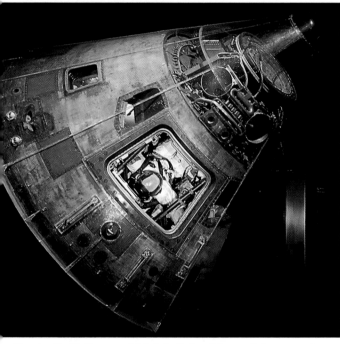

*The rocket-powered X-15 bridged the gap between flight in the atmosphere and flight into space. (SI no. 79-833)*

*The Apollo 11 Command Module* Columbia *carried astronauts Armstrong, Aldrin, and Collins to the Moon and back in July 1969. (SI no. 80-4978)*

bols of human, rather than technological, achievement—the first international agreement to ban an entire class of nuclear missiles (those having a range of 500–5500 kilometers or 300–3400 miles).

In a unique "nuclear exchange," the Smithsonian Institution and the government of the Soviet Union agreed to exhibit these missiles—the most powerful and threatening of the weapons to be eliminated under the treaty—here in Washington, D.C., and at the Central Armed Forces Museum in Moscow.

The **North American X-15** spearheaded research in a variety of aerospace areas, including hypersonic aerodynamics, winged reentry from space, and life-support systems for spacecraft. It spanned the gap between flight in the atmosphere and flight into space; eight of its pilots qualified for astronaut's wings by exceeding an 80-kilometer (50-mile) altitude on an X-15 flight.

Historic manned spacecraft are also displayed in this gallery. Space exploration was envisioned by early rocket pioneers such as Dr. Robert H. Goddard, whose work was supported in part by the Smithsonian Institution. Goddard flew the world's first successful liquid-propellant rocket on March 16, 1926; here on display is a full-scale model of that rocket and one of his later rockets, dating to 1941.

Also on display is John Glenn's **"Friendship 7"**, which is separated from the Wright Flyer by six meters (less than 20 feet) and only 59 years in time. During this Project Mercury mission, Glenn became the first American astronaut to orbit the Earth. Nearby is the two-seat **Gemini 4** spacecraft, from which

Edward H. White ventured on the first "space walk" by a U.S. astronaut. The **Apollo 11 Command Module "Columbia"** carried astronauts Neil Armstrong, Edwin Aldrin, and Michael Collins to the Moon and back, completing history's first manned lunar landing mission in July 1969.

You will see important unmanned spacecraft in this gallery. The Russian **Sputnik 1** satellite (the replica of the first artificial satellite to orbit the Earth, October 4, 1957), and **Explorer 1** satellite (backup model of the first U.S. satellite to orbit the Earth, January 31, 1958) provided the impetus for the many U.S. space missions that followed them. The significance of Sputnik 1 can hardly be overestimated. This mission triggered a number of important events in the United States, including the establishment of the National Aeronautics and Space Administration and the enactment by Congress of the National Defense Education Act of 1958. Following the successful launch by the Soviet Union of Sputniks 1 and 2, and delays in the American Vanguard program, the United States launched its first artificial satellite—Explorer 1. It made the first major scientific discovery of the space age, detecting radiation belts around Earth.

A replica **Mariner 2** is also on display. Mariner 2 was the first successful interplanetary probe to explore the environment of another planet on December 14, 1962. Mariner 2 flew within 34,800 kilometers (20,800 miles) of the planet Venus, and began transmitting information back to Earth, 58 million kilometers (36 million miles) away. **Pioneer 10** con-

*The Douglas M-2 Mailplane was one of the first airmail and passenger aircraft. Western Air Express flew this M-2 from 1926 to 1930 on a mail route from Los Angeles to Salt Lake City. (SI no. 80-2101)*

ducted the first flyby exploration of an outer planet of our solar system (Pioneer 10 sent back images of Jupiter on December 10, 1972, and continued out beyond the orbits of Neptune and Pluto). The craft on display is a prototype for the actual Pioneer 10. The **Viking Lander** was the first U.S. spacecraft to view Mars, and from its own surface. Viking also conducted scientific tests on soil samples to determine the composition of the soil and to look for evidence of life.

**Don't Miss** the moonrock sample: you can touch this specimen of basaltic material from the surface of the Moon. Four billion years old, it is a small bit of the 109 kilometers (243 pounds) of lunar samples brought back to Earth by the Apollo 17 astronauts on December 19, 1972.

### Air Transportation (Gallery 102)

This gallery contains representative air-craft used by the pioneer airlines during the evolution of air transport in the United States. From 1926 to 1936—no more than one decade—commercial aircraft progressed from the open cockpit mailplane to the 21-seat ancestor of the jet airliners we know today. The transport aircraft displayed in this gallery helped lay the foundations for the airlines of the United States and their expansion into worldwide air routes.

The **Douglas M-2** was one of the first airmail (and occasional passenger) aircraft. Western Air Express flew it from 1926 to 1930 on a mail route from Los Angeles to Salt Lake City. Its pilot, helmeted, goggled, and swathed in a long leather flying coat, sat in the rearmost open cockpit. Two passengers sometimes shared the frigid forward cockpit with bags of mail. The trip took six hours and cost $90.

Pitcairn Aviation, Inc. (which became Eastern Airlines) flew this **Mailwing** be-

*Above*: This Pitcairn Mailwing delivered mail between New York and Atlanta during the 1920s and 1930s. It was the first Mailwing ever built. (SI no. 80-2095) **Bottom photo**: The all-metal Ford Tri-Motor was extremely popular at the time of its design in the late 1920s. (SI no. 80-2104)

*The Northrop Alpha is remarkable for the strong yet light design of its multicellular wing, which is still used by aircraft designers today. (SI no. 80-2100)*

tween New York and Atlanta, with intermediate stops in Philadelphia, Baltimore, Washington, and Richmond. This was the first Mailwing ever built, and is of the same era as the Douglas M-2.

Passenger travel was a logical outgrowth of flights using the network of airmail routes linking major cities. The **Fairchild FC-2**, a utility aircraft built during the late 1920s, was designed to carry four passengers, and was typical of the small, single-engine types of its time. Built mainly of wood and strong fabric, it was nevertheless a versatile machine, and served the airlines during the cold winters of the Canadian north and the hot summers of South American deserts. This particular aircraft, owned by PANAGRA, a Pan American affiliate, inaugurated the first service along the South American west coast in 1928.

The **Ford Tri-Motor** was extremely popular at the time of its design in the late 1920s. Although noisy and drafty, the Tri-Motor was relatively comfortable. Its all-metal body and three engines did much to reassure the nervous air traveler, as did Henry Ford's reputation for reliability. American Airways flew this Tri-Motor (a 5-AT-B model) on a transcontinental route during the early 1930s. Years later, American Airlines (successors to Airways) found it near a small Mexican airfield, where it had been converted into living quarters. American Airlines then restored the aircraft to flying condition.

The sleek, single-engine **Northrop Alpha** carried passengers in an enclosed cabin, along with 465 pounds (209 kilograms) of mail; curiously, the pilot still sat outside in an open cockpit. It is remarkable for the strong yet light design of its multicellular wing, which is still used by aircraft designers today. The Alpha was used mainly for flying experimental routes, and was retired from service in the mid-1930s.

The **Boeing 247-D** was the refinement of the first truly modern airliner. The 247, a derivative of the Model 200 Monomail and B-9 bomber, showed a

*The DC-3's streamlined, versatile design and strong wing construction make it an exceptional aircraft. It dominates the Hall of Air Transportation, the heaviest craft—at 17,500 pounds—to hang from the Museum's ceiling. (NASM photo)*

substantial improvement over the Ford Tri-Motor, cutting eight hours from the coast-to-coast flying time, and was capable of carrying 10 people. The Museum's 247-D flew in the famous England-to-Australia air race of 1934.

Also on exhibit here is a **Douglas DC-3**—a descendant of the DC-1, which was TWA's answer to United's Boeing 247. The DC-1 incorporated Jack Northrop's multicellular wing construction and light yet powerful engines, and carried 12 passengers in relative comfort. The DC-2 production model that followed has 14 seats. The 21-seat DC-3, later able to accommodate 28 or more passengers, was originally designed as a sleeper—the DST—to carry passengers overnight from New York to Los Angeles. With a full load, it was the first transport airplane that could fly passengers without mail and still make a profit. The DC-3's streamlined, versatile design and strong wing construction made it an exceptional aircraft; at least 400 of these airplanes are still flying today.

The **Grumman G-21 Amphibian** was the first commercial design for Grumman Aircraft Engineering Corporation. First flown in May 1937, the G-21 was considered especially safe: any body of water could be used as an emergency landing field, the hull was all metal and sturdy, and the engines, two Pratt & Whitney "Wasp Juniors," had a reputation for reliability. Over a half century, the "Goose," originally an aerial limousine designed for a wealthy few, has evolved into a hardworking hauler of passengers and freight.

*This gallery documents the results of our efforts to attain vertical flight with helicopters, autogiros, and other specially designed vehicles. (NASM photo)*

## Vertical Flight (Gallery 103)

Here are the results of human efforts to attain vertical flight—helicopters, autogiros, and other specially designed vehicles. The drawings, photographs, and models in this gallery show what these vehicles had in common: a rotating airscrew or wing, mounted to produce downward thrust or lift. The result is today's now-familiar helicopter rotor assembly with two or more revolving blades. The blades are rotary wings that provide lift, and function the same way as fixed wings of a conventional airplane.

Autogiros, like the **Kellett XO-60**, were a step toward achieving the goal of vertical flight. Unlike a helicopter, the rotor of an autogiro is not powered; it turns freely in the air. The autogiro has to be moving forward in order for the rotor to turn. Developed for the U.S. Army in 1942, the Kellett XO-60 could land nearly vertically, and could lift off after a very short takeoff run.

The Focke-Achgelis company began constructing the **Focke-Achgelis FA-330** in the fall of 1941, in response to the German Navy's need for greater long-range visibility of surfaced U-boats. This new autogiro, a piloted kite with rotating wings, was designed to carry one observer/pilot, and was pulled along behind the submarine by a cable. The FA-330 was equipped with a telephone, which allowed the pilot to communicate with individuals on the boat.

The **Piasecki PV-2** first took off on April 11, 1943, flown by designer Frank Piasecki. It was the second helicopter to be successfully flown in the United States. The first helicopter to be mass-produced in the United States was the **Sikorsky XR-4**. Its medical evacuation missions in Burma during World War II pioneered that highly important use of

20

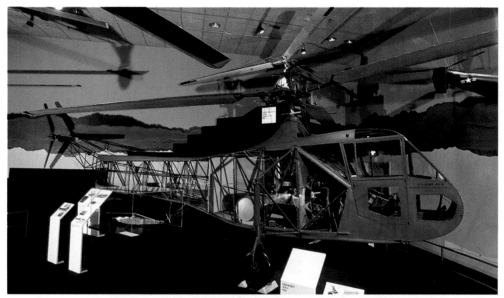

*The Sikorsky XR-4 was the first helicopter to be mass-produced in the United States. (NASM photo)*

*Designed specifically for antisubmarine warfare, its outstanding performance quickly proved the Sikorsky UH-34D suitable for other military services. In 1961, a Marine UH-34D picked up astronaut Alan Shepard following his splashdown in* Freedom 7. *(NASM photo)*

rotary-winged craft. A direct descendant of the Sikorsky XR-4, this **UH-34D Sea Horse** carried Marine assault troops in Vietnam, and now dominates this gallery. Also on display is the **Bell 206L-1 LongRanger II "Spirit of Texas,"** which became the first helicopter to be flown around the world, in September 1982.

*In September 1982, H. Ross Perot, Jr. and Jay Coburn flew their Bell 206L-1 LongRanger II* Spirit of Texas *in the first around-the-world helicopter flight. (SI no. 91-15701)*

Stanley Hiller, Jr., designed the bright yellow **Hiller helicopter** in 1942, at the age of 17. His goals were to eliminate the tail rotor, and to make the helicopter easier to operate. The result of his efforts was the first successful U.S. helicopter with coaxial, counterrotating blades.

In 1954 Igor Bensen developed his one-man **Gyro-Glider**, which was designed to take two men two weeks to construct. No pilot's license was required to operate this craft. Lightweight and portable, the Gyro-Glider was designed to be towed behind a small automobile for take off at 25 miles (40 kilometers) per hour. With winds above that speed, the aircraft could lift off by itself, like a kite. Bensen's **Gyro-Copter**, flown in December of 1955, was a powered

version of the Gyro-Glider.

Individual lifting devices have been tested for military use and for personal transportation. One design was Horace T. Pentecost's **Pentecost Hoppicopter**, an 88-pound (40-kilogram) rotary-wing back pack, shown here on the mannequin of a Marine. Developed during World War II, this air machine was designed for army paratroopers and was intended to supplant the clumsy parachute. The Hoppicopter's frailty was human; legs were not designed to be landing-gear. Despite refinements in its design, the original Hoppicopter concept gave way to existing lightweight helicopter designs.

Two of the superb cutaway models here underscore the complexity of the mechanisms of vertical flight. One is a **Pratt & Whitney PT6-T** turboshaft engine installed in a partial nose section of a Sikorsky S-58T. The second is a **cockpit and rotor system model**, its inner workings exposed so that the visitor can follow the intricacies of the hand- and foot-operated controls.

**Don't Miss** the Cayley Convertiplane model.

**Special Aircraft Exhibits (Gallery 104)**
Installed here are changing exhibits highlighting significant aircraft from various periods in the development of heavier-than-air flight. Check with the information desk on the current exhibit.

**Golden Age of Flight (Gallery 105)**
Perhaps the most exciting years of aviation history span the period from the end of World War I to our entry into World War II. This period is referred to as "golden" because of the countless advances in aviation technology that occurred, the many expeditions undertaken, and the numerous records set. In this gallery, the visitor gains a sense of the major progress made in aviation during this time.

In the Golden Age of Flight, the public was intensely interested in aviation events. The names of air-race pilots and aerobatic flyers were constantly in the headlines and newsreels. Here are race programs from the 1920s and 1930s, along with air race tickets, grandstand passes, and other interesting memorabilia of the time. Another display case contains aircraft models, trophies, and air-race information.

Lured by the fascination of far-off lands, the adventurous aviator of the Golden Age ventured to the jungles of New Guinea and the Amazon, and to the uncharted polar regions. Here is the **Northrop Gamma "Polar Star,"** in a recreated south polar landscape. Lincoln Ellsworth and his pilot, Herbert Hollick-Kenyon, flew this aircraft across the Antarctic in 1935. The visitor can also learn about the polar explorations of Richard E. Byrd and Bernt Balchen from an informative wall display.

Countless important aircraft flew during the Golden Age. **The Beech Model C17L Staggerwing** earned its name from the placement of its lower wing ahead of the upper. The aircraft first flew in 1932, and became popular for luxury private and business transport. Steve Wittman's red **"Buster"** enjoyed perhaps the longest and most successful career of any aircraft in racing history. Wittman took numerous trophies for race records flying *Buster* before retiring it in 1954. On exhibit is the **Curtiss Robin "Ole Miss,"** which the Key brothers of Meridian, Mississippi, flew to set a world record for sustained flight (approximately 27 days).

During the 1920s and 1930s, the U.S. Navy acquired a number of aircraft and experimented with various ways to adapt aircraft to naval usage. The photos and models exhibited here show how the Navy accomplished this. A similar display illustrates the growth

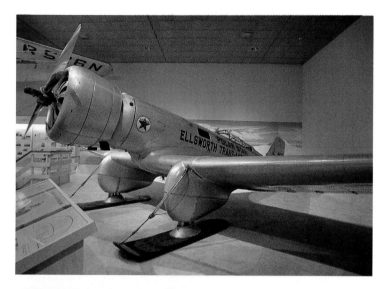

*Explorer Lincoln Ellsworth and his pilot, Herbert Hollick-Kenyon, flew the Northrop* Gamma Polar Star *across the Antarctic in 1935. (NASM photo)*

*The* Wittman Buster *enjoyed perhaps the longest and most successful career of any aircraft in racing history. (NASM photo)*

*Howard Hughes built his sleek H-1 Racer and flew it to speed records in 1935 and 1937. (NASM photo)*

*The Key brothers set a world record for sustained flight (approximately 27 days) in the Curtiss Robin J-1 Ole Miss. (NASM photo)*

and development of the Army Air Corps and its theory of strategic bombardment during this time.

**Don't Miss** the Golden Age Theater. Here, Jimmy Doolittle reminisces about aviation in that era.

### Jet Aviation (Gallery 106)

This gallery focuses on the development and present state of jet aviation and its related technology.

Two college students in their early twenties, one English and one German, were key figures in the development of jet aviation. Flight Cadet Frank Whittle, Royal Air Force College, Cranwell, wrote his final thesis in 1928, when he was 21; it contained the germ of the idea of jet propulsion for aircraft. Hans Joachim Pabst von Ohain began his research on a gas turbine propulsion system in 1933, when he was 22 and in his seventh semester at the University of Goettingen.

Working independently, these men arrived at their chosen goals: building and testing the world's first jet engines for aircraft propulsion. Von Ohain's jet engine flew first, in a Heinkel He 178, on August 27, 1939. Whittle's flew in a Gloster E28/39 on May 15, 1941. In this gallery, giant engines dwarf the visitor, contemporary reminders of their successes.

Under the pressures of World War II, development of the jet engine was channeled into military aircraft programs. The new powerplants promised higher speeds and altitudes—characteristics that the Germans desperately sought to counter the Allied bomber attacks. Quite naturally, the first jet-propelled warplane in combat was a German design—the **Messerschmitt Me 262A-Schwalbe** (swallow).

The Museum's **Lockheed XP-80 Shooting Star "Lulu Belle"** is the prototype for the United States's first opera-

*The Messerschmitt Me 262 was the first jet-propelled warplane used in combat. (NASM photo)*

*The Lockheed XP-80 Shooting Star* Lulu Belle *is the prototype for the United States's first operational jet fighter. (NASM photo)*

*The McDonnell FH-1 Phantom was the first U.S. carrier-based jet aircraft. (SI no. 43302)*

tional jet fighter. Developed under wartime conditions of secrecy and urgency by a hand-picked team of 128 individuals, the *Lulu Belle* flew for the first time on January 8, 1944, fewer than seven months after the Army Air Forces signed a contract with Lockheed. This craft appeared too late to fight in World War II, but bore the brunt of early combat in Korea a few years later.

The first U.S. carrier-based jet aircraft, the McDonnell **FH-1 Phantom I**, took off from and landed on the deck of the USS *Franklin D. Roosevelt* on July 21, 1946. The tradition of that first Phantom is carried on today by McDonnell Douglas's F-4 Phantom II, now in worldwide service.

A mural by artist Keith Ferris serves as a dramatic backdrop for this gallery; Ferris included many of the important jet aircraft developed since Hans von Ohain's pioneering effort in 1939.

**Don't Miss** the comedy film *Sneaking through the Sound Barrier*, starring Sid Caesar and Imogene Coca.

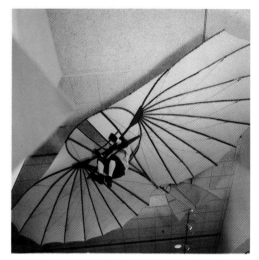

*Many important jet aircraft are included in Keith Ferris's mural, which serves as a dramatic backdrop for this gallery. (NASM photo)*

### Early Flight (Gallery 107)

Experience the early history of the airplane—from some of the earliest notions of flying, through the first decade of powered flight. This gallery evokes the mood and excitement of a time when wings were new by depicting a 1913 aeronautical trade show. The labels are written as if it were 1913, to give the visitor a sense of how the achievements of the Wright brothers and other innovators were first introduced to the public.

When Otto Lilienthal built his **Lilienthal Hang-Glider** in 1894, he considered it the safest and most successful of all his glider designs. In flight, the pilot hung between the wings by bars that passed beneath his arms. Lilienthal made glides of up to 1,150 feet (345 meters) in machines of this type. Despite

*Otto Lilienthal made glides of up to 1,150 feet (345 meters) in his Lilienthal gliders. (NASM photo)*

*Above*: The Wright 1909 Military Flyer was the world's first military airplane. *(NASM photo)* **Bottom photo**: The Curtiss Headless Pusher was well suited to exhibition flying because of its maneuverability and ease of assembly. *(NASM photo)*

Lilienthal's faith in the safety of his invention, he met his death following a crash in a hang-glider similar to the one exhibited here.

His efforts were not in vain, however, for two young men named Orville and Wilbur Wright read about Lilienthal's experiments and were inspired to tackle the problem of heavier-than-air flight themselves. In 1899, they wrote to the Smithsonian Institution for information about experiments that had been conducted up to that time.

Samuel P. Langley, third Secretary of the Smithsonian Institution, constructed this quarter-scale model of the **Aerodrome** in 1901. It was one of seven such unmanned powered aircraft he built and flew at the turn of the century. Some had steam engines, others were gasoline powered. He used this model for balance studies when designing and constructing the full-scale, man-carrying Aerodrome A of 1903. The Quarter-Scale Aerodrome flew twice on June 18, 1901, covering distances of 150 feet (45 meters) and 300 feet (90 meters). Its final flight was on August 8, 1903, when it traveled a distance of 1,000 feet (300 meters).

The **1909 Wright Military Flyer** was the world's first military airplane. In 1908, the U.S. Army Signal Corps ordered a two-seat observation aircraft—one that was relatively simple to operate, could reach a speed of at least 40 miles (64 kilometers) per hour in still air, and could remain in the air for at least one hour without landing. The Army also required that the aircraft be easy to assemble and disassemble and be able to land safely and take off quickly. In the fall of 1909, Orville Wright successfully met the Signal Corps's specifications with this airplane, and the military gained its wings. The War Department presented this Wright Military Flyer to the Smithsonian Institution in 1911.

Lincoln Beachey, and other noted Curtiss Aircraft test and exhibition pilots, flew the **Curtiss Model D "Headless Pusher"** because it gave excellent performance, especially in the hands of an experienced pilot. The Curtiss D and E aircraft were suited to exhibition flying not only because of their maneuverability, but also because of their easy disassembly and reassembly for shipment between exhibition dates. This 1912-style example was built by Glen Curtiss after World War I for nostalgic reasons. The Model D, first manufactured in 1909, was dubbed the "Headless Pusher" because of its lack of a forward elevator surface. Earlier versions had both a rear and forward elevator.

Herman Ecker epitomized the pioneer spirit of the new aerial age with his **Ecker Flying Boat**. Inspired by the Wright brothers and Glenn Curtiss, Ecker learned to fly in 1911, built his own aeroplane, and made his living as an exhibition pilot. Ecker originally designed his aircraft with wheels so that it could take off from land. In 1912, he fitted the craft with pontoons, which allowed it to take off from, and alight on, water. Ecker constructed his Flying Boat largely from common materials found in local hardware stores.

Frenchman Louis Blériot's **Blériot XI** was the most popular pre-World War I monoplane. The example exhibited here is very similar to the aircraft he used on July 25, 1909, to make the first heavier-than-air flight across the English Channel. Taking off from the dunes near Calais and landing beside Dover Castle, he made the 23-mile (37-kilometer) flight in 37 minutes at an average speed of 36 miles (58 kilometers) per hour. The single-seat Blériot XI was capable of remaining in the air for up to three hours and could climb to 1,640 feet (492 meters) in five minutes.

Also on exhibit in gallery 107 are a variety of **aeronautical engines**—the in-line, radial, and rotary powerplants that propelled the first airplanes.

**Don't Miss** the "Early Birds" Plaque, which lists the members of the "Early Birds," an international organization, created in 1928, of pilots who flew before December 17, 1916. An accompanying film shown in the gallery includes priceless motion picture footage that highlights the early history of aviation. Glenn Curtiss's pilot's license is also on display here.

### Independence Avenue Lobby (Gallery 108)

Two dramatic murals dominate the walls of the Independence Avenue Lobby. **Space Mural—A Cosmic View** was painted by Robert T. McCall on the east side of the lobby in 1976. The L-shaped mural's horizontal section is 75 feet in length; the vertical section stretches 58 feet, 6 inches. The mural's story unfolds from the left, starting with the artist's depiction of the birth of the universe. The viewer is carried past planets and asteroids. Dominating the center portion of the mural is an American astronaut on the surface of the Moon, with the lunar module, a second astronaut, and the lunar rover in the background. Orbiting above are the command and service modules. The vertical section depicts the rising Sun, galaxies, and the Milky Way.

*Above:* Space Mural—A Cosmic View *is Robert McCall's version of the beginnings of our universe. (NASM photo)* **Bottom photo**: *Earthflight Environment is Eric Sloane's representation of the remarkable ocean of air that is our environment. (NASM photo)*

On the west wall of the lobby, also painted in 1976, is **Earth Flight Environment**, by artist Eric Sloan. This painting, also L-shaped (and 75 feet by 58 feet, 6 inches), shows a panoramic view of a western landscape as a lone airplane streaks across the sky. On the left the painting changes from realistic to symbolic. Lightning, rain, a rainbow, and an assortment of cloud formations rise toward a rocket airplane. Finally, at the top of the vertical segment, there is a depiction of the aurora borealis, and the stars of space. The border at the bottom of the mural is decorated with a variety of weather map symbols.

The **Voyager**, first aircraft to complete a non-stop, non-refueled round-the-world flight, is suspended above the information desk. The main engine, the Teledyne Continental I0L-200, is on exhibit nearby.

## Flight Testing (Gallery 109)

Flight testing began as an engineering discipline soon after World War I, encompassing research on the ground and in the air. Early tests at the Army's McCook Field, Dayton, Ohio, probed the uncertainties of contemporary aircraft and evaluated some of the combat types that had flown in the war. Soon, flight testing emerged as a specialty in the broadening field of aeronautical science.

Flight researcher Wiley Post's early experiments with pressure suits led direct-

*Above: Flight researcher Wiley Post flew the Lockheed 5C Vega* Winnie Mae *to the unheard-of height of 50,000 feet (15,240 meters) while pursuing research for the pressure flight suit. (SI no. 80-2083)* **Bottom photo***: Voyager is the first aircraft to fly around the world without landing or refueling. The nine-day, 25,012-mile flight took place in December, 1986. Voyager carried 1,209 gallons (7.012 pounds) of fuel at take-off. The aircraft is virtually without metal parts, composed primarily of a quarter-inch thick sandwich of resin-treated paper honeycomb and carbon graphite fiber. Its main fuselage contains a cabin cockpit measuring just 7$\frac{1}{2}$ feet long and 3$\frac{1}{2}$ feet wide. (NASM photo)*

ly to the astronaut garments of today. In 1934, Post unofficially flew this **Lockheed 5C Vega "Winnie Mae"** to the unbelievable height of 50,000 feet (15,240 meters) while pursuing research for the pressure suit. Also on exhibit is the **Bell XP-59A Airacomet**, the first U.S. turbojet aircraft. Designed in response to an Army request for a jet-propelled fighter, the XP-59A first flew on October 1, 1942. It was a disappointment, however; the aircraft performed poorly, the engines did not deliver the promised thrust, and the aircraft was not a stable gunnery platform.

The **Hawker Siddeley XV-6A Kestrel** represents a highly innovative and successful approach to vertical flight. The ability to vector the thrust of the aircraft's exhaust enabled the Kestrel to make vertical and short takeoffs and landings. The National Aeronautics and Space Administration (NASA) used the Kestrel for basic investigations of vertical flight from 1968 through 1974; it is the predecessor of the current Harrier.

## Looking at Earth (Gallery 110)

Photos, cameras, sensors, aircraft, and spacecraft are combined here in tracing the development of aerial and orbital imagery of the Earth. This gallery demonstrates how the technology of Earth observation grew along with the technology of flight, progressing from early experiments with balloons and kites to techniques for imaging from orbit.

*The Hawker Siddeley Kestrel, a vertical takeoff and landing aircraft, represents a highly innovative and successful approach to vertical flight. (SI no. 80-13716)*

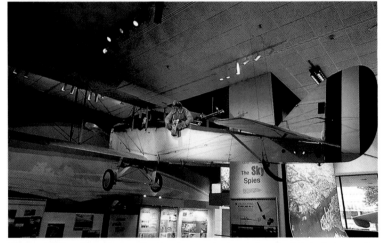

*Above: This gallery traces the development of aerial and orbital photography. (SI no. 86-6033)* **Bottom photo**: *The de Havilland DH-4 played an important role in aerial photography during World War I and in the 1920s. (SI no. 86-6029)*

Drawing on the resources of the Museum's diverse research departments, *Looking at Earth* provides a wide variety of information highlighting both the history and science of Earth observations.

Today, aircraft and spacecraft provide imagery useful for predicting the weather, surveying terrain, monitoring crops and forests, planning cities, locating resources, and gathering intelligence. The exhibition is divided into a number of sections, the first of which is "A Bird's-Eye View." The viewer begins by examining photographs taken from low-altitude balloons and kites. Examples include the first American panorama taken from a balloon, in Boston in 1860; a 1908 photo of pigeons with strapped-on mini-metrogon cameras; and the photo of San Francisco taken after the 1906 earthquake, by a camera carried aloft by 17 kites. Civil War balloon observations are highlighted by memorabilia of the balloon pioneer, Thaddeus Lowe.

The following section, "Up, Up and Away," describes more modern applications of balloon and blimp photography, including the **Skyhook** camera (which was part of a reconnaissance mission over the Soviet Union), the Explorer II high altitude research balloon (photo only), and views from a Goodyear blimp.

"Onwards and Upwards" highlights airplane photography, and the two aircraft exhibited in the gallery illustrate the rapid advances made in the technology of looking at Earth. In addition to being used as a bomber in World War I, the **de Havilland DH-4** also functioned as an observation and photo reconnaissance craft. After the war, the U.S. Army Air Service used the DH-4 for a variety of purposes, including forest patrols, geologic reconnaissance, and aerial photography.

The open-cockpit DH-4 presents a dramatic contrast with the **Lockheed U-2** high-altitude reconnaissance aircraft, designed only some 40 years later. The U-2 has played a vital role in reconnaissance of the Soviet missile buildup in Cuba, verification of nuclear testing in China, reconnaissance in Vietnam and the Middle East, and resource and atmospheric monitoring.

*The Lockheed U-2 has been an important aerial mapping and surveillance craft since the 1950s. (NASM photo)*

"The Changing Landscape" demonstrates how aerial photography enables urban planners, resource managers, conservationists, and historians to view changes in the land through time. Here we see the dramatic changes that occurred in the flow of the Big Sioux river in South Dakota; through the years, portions of the river were changed from a winding and sinuous pattern to a straight and unbending one. These photos vividly document the attempts made by Sioux Falls residents to control floods and monitor changes in the river.

"The Sky Spies" illustrates the use of aerial photography in gathering military intelligence. Photointerpreters and reconnaissance pilots play a vital role in this area. These individuals used aerial intelligence for assignments during both World Wars, during the Cuban Missile Crisis, and for countless other military endeavors. The **Discoverer 13** satellite also supplied reconnaissance photography. Discoverer 13 was launched on August 10, 1960, and its reentry pod was the first man-made object recovered from space.

"Orbital Vistas—The Earth from Space" shows useful as well as beautiful satellite views of familiar sites such as the Grand Canyon and Death Valley. Call up a Landsat scene of your home state on a videodisc and see yourself as a satellite might see you on a special television screen. A nearby computer display explains some basics of satellite sensing.

Nearby is the weather station "A Satellite for All Seasons." Images from weather satellites do more than just aid in the forecasting process. They allow us to observe current weather conditions and trace and predict atmospheric circulation patterns. Learn about **TIROS** (Television and Infrared Observation Satellite)—the world's first weather satellite. TIROS satellites have provided thousands of images of Earth from orbit, and revolutionized the science of storm prediction. A full-scale model of a **GOES** (Geostationary Operational Environmental Satellite) is also on display. GOES satellites are designed to monitor constantly the same region of the Earth. From its geostationary orbit, a GOES provides thorough coverage of a region's daily weather developments, as well as early warning of severe storms. Today's GOES is equipped with additional instruments to measure atmospheric temperature and solar activity. Watch the screen to see information on daily weather conditions as monitored by GOES.

"What's New?," an exhibit at the gallery's exit, highlights the latest developments in the rapidly advancing field of Earth monitoring. The visitor can see imagery from recent experiments and missions as well as photos of new U.S. and international spacecraft developed for Earth observations.

*TIROS (Television and Infrared Observation Satellite) is the world's first weather satellite. (SI no. 86-6053)*

*GOES (Geostationary Operational Environmental Satellite) provides intense coverage of a region's daily weather developments and early warning of severe storms. (NASM photo)*

*The visitor learns about the cultural importance of the Sun and stars in this gallery. (NASM photo)*

*The Aerobee Nose Cone is equipped with sun-seeker pointing controls. On the left is an OSO (Orbiting Solar Observatory), which NASA designed to observe the Sun in ultraviolet, X-ray, and gamma-ray regions of the spectrum. (NASM photo)*

*The Apollo Telescope Mount from Skylab (left center) exhibited in this gallery contained a variety of instruments to study the Sun. To the Apollo Telescope Mount's right are the Aerobee Nose Cone and the OSO. (NASM photo)*

## Stars (Gallery 111)

The National Air and Space Museum has the world's largest and most comprehensive collection of scientific instruments for observing the Sun and stars from space. During your walk through the Stars gallery, you will see artifacts from major historical periods in the development of X-ray, ultraviolet, visible, and infrared astronomy.

A **scale model of Stonehenge** illustrates how the gigantic monoliths were probably used to determine the positions of sunrise and the passage of the seasons. Ancient Britons most likely used Stonehenge as a horizon calendar. After examining the Stonehenge model, turn the corner, and you will confront an imposing array of spacecraft used to observe the Sun, stars, our galaxy, and the universe.

The **Aerobee Nose Cone** on display here is equipped with sun-seeker pointing controls. These controls enabled the Aerobee rocket to point its instruments directly toward the Sun, even as the rocket turned and gyrated in space. The SOLRAD series of satellites helped scientists to understand the complex character of the Earth's upper atmosphere, and how it is influenced by solar radiation. **SOLRAD 1**, a mock-up of which is on display here, orbited the Earth to continuously monitor the Sun's X-ray and gamma-ray output.

On March 7, 1962, NASA launched the first of its **Orbiting Solar Observatories** (OSOs); we see an example of an OSO satellite next to the Aerobee nosecone. NASA designed OSO to observe the Sun in ultraviolet, X-ray, and gamma-ray regions of the spectrum. In order to maintain stability, OSO's three protruding arms spun around the central core, like a gyroscope, as it traveled around the Earth.

Scientists used Skylab to observe and gather important data about the Sun. The backup **Apollo Telescope Mount** from Skylab exhibited here contained a variety of instruments to study the Sun.

Inside **Skylab**, the astronauts operated the telescopes by remote control; they made several trips outside to change film cassettes. The Skylab telescopes showed the Sun in visible light, in ultraviolet light, and in X-rays.

When we look far away into space, we see into the past. In the center of the gallery you will be able to find the approximate position of your "birthday star." When you enter your age on the keyboard, the name of that star on the chart will appear along with its distance in light years. The light we now see from that star in the real sky left its surface at about the time you were born.

Examine **Uhuru**, the first X-ray astronomy satellite. Exhibited here is a full-scale rebuilt satellite. Uhuru (which means "freedom" in Swahili) was launched from an off-shore platform in Kenya on the seventh anniversary of Kenyan independence, December 12, 1970. It provided scientists with important data about galaxies and quasars, and demonstrated the feasibility of X-ray astronomy in space.

Since the invention of the first crude telescope in the early 17th century, we have explored the sky with ground-based instruments. Why should we travel into space to conduct astronomical observations? You will find the answer to this question in the Stars gallery. Panels reveal how traditional reflecting and refracting telescopes collect, focus, and analyze starlight, and how space telescopes have to do the very same things. Telescopes located on Earth are limited by its atmosphere, which distorts and blocks most of the light of the Sun and stars. So scientists have sought to rise above Earth's atmosphere, to view the heavens from space. Today, astronomical instruments on aircraft, balloons, and spacecraft allow us to investigate new regions of the spectrum.

A telescope's primary function is to collect light. Both ground-based and space telescopes perform the same function—they focus light (whether it is ultraviolet or infrared) onto detectors, where the light is recorded. Unlike the ground-based models, space telescopes must essentially be robots, able to take care of themselves. Unless they are specially designed for servicing by Space Shuttle astronauts, it is not feasible to repair space telescopes after they are launched.

The **Hubble Space Telescope** (HST) was launched by the Space Shuttle *Discovery* in April 1990, and is the largest astronomical instrument in space. Because of a manufacturing error, the HST's primary mirror produces images that are not properly focused. However, the HST is still a powerful astronomical tool. It has been designed to be maintained and repaired in the Space Shuttle. A 1/5-scale model of the HST hangs at the gallery's entrance, and items related to the Telescope are displayed at the rear of the gallery. A full-scale engineering model is on display in Space Hall.

Scientists have made surveys of the infrared sky from high mountains, from balloons, and from aircraft. NASA has modified several aircraft to fly at high altitudes in order to observe the infrared (or heat radiation) energy received from celestial objects. An infrared telescope designed in the early 1960s was placed in an open port of a Lear jet, and was flown regularly at an altitude of 13.5 kilometers (45,000 feet).

After experimenting with high-flying aircraft, scientists were ready to survey the entire sky from space, completely above the obscuring atmosphere. The result was the **Infrared Astronomical Satellite** (IRAS). This spacecraft was the culmination of experiments conducted by the prototype Caltech Infrared Telescope seen in this gallery, and other infrared programs. Launched on January 24, 1983, IRAS carried a highly sensitive infrared telescope and a unique liquid-helium system to cool its detectors and the optics to about -271 degrees centigrade (-455 degrees Fahrenheit). Such low operating temperatures allowed the telescope to measure the heat from stars and other celestial objects. By the time it had run out of its supply of super-cold liquid helium 10 months later, IRAS had observed 98 percent of the sky in each of the four infrared bands.

The **Caltech Infrared Telescope** is one of the founding instruments of infrared astronomy. Designed in the 1960s by

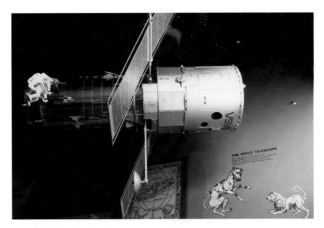

*The Hubble Space Telescope, the largest astronomical telescope in space, was launched aboard the Space Shuttle* Discovery *in April 1990. This is a $\frac{1}{5}$-scale model. (NASM photo)*

*The International Ultraviolet Explorer spacecraft (IUE) was launched on January 26, 1978, into a high orbit around the Earth. It carries a 45-centimeter (17.7 inch) reflecting telescope with a spectrograph that senses ultraviolet light. (NASM photo)*

*On July 28, 1964, the Ranger 7 Lunar Probe transmitted 4,316 high-quality pictures of the Moon to scientists on Earth. (NASA)*

California Institute of Technology scientists, this ground-based telescope conducted the first survey of the sky in the infrared, opening a new era in astronomical exploration.

**Don't Miss** "The Powers of Ten" and "How Big Are Stars?" displays.

### Lunar Exploration Vehicles (Gallery 112)

In 1961, President John F. Kennedy committed the United States to "the goal, before this decade is out, of landing a man on the Moon and returning him safely to the Earth." As a result, NASA developed a variety of lunar exploration spacecraft to take photographs of and map the Moon's surface in an effort to find a suitable landing site for future manned missions. These unmanned lunar probes were **Ranger, Lunar Orbiter**, and **Surveyor.**

Launched from Cape Canaveral, Florida, on July 28, 1964, the **Ranger 7 Lunar Probe** took high-quality pictures of the lunar surface, transmitting 4,316 of them to scientists on Earth. Scientists estimated that they were 1,000 times better than the best photographs then available from Earth-based telescopes.

The spacecraft **Surveyor** followed Ranger in examining the lunar surface. Unlike Ranger, which crashed on the Moon's surface, Surveyor made a soft-landing on the Moon and operated for extended periods of time directly on the Moon's surface. NASA launched Surveyor 1 from the Kennedy Space Center on May 30, 1966. Six more launches followed, five of which accomplished the goals set forth for the program. Surveyor 3, equipped with a scoop and claw

*Surveyor made a soft-landing on the Moon and operated for extended periods of time directly on the Moon's surface. (NASM photo)*

*Lunar Orbiters like this one were equipped with self-contained photographic laboratories, and provided detailed maps of most of the Moon's surface. (NASM photo)*

device, tested the cohesiveness of the lunar surface and placed samples in front of the spacecraft's camera; Surveyor 5 carried an instrument that could analyze the surface material chemically. Surveyor 7 was equipped with both devices. Like Ranger, all the Surveyors relayed images of the Moon's surface by way of a television system.

The remaining unmanned lunar probes were the five **Lunar Orbiters**, which provided detailed maps of most of the Moon's surface. Unlike the Ranger and Surveyor television system, the Lunar Orbiters carried self-contained photographic laboratories. The systems snapped the pictures, developed the film, and scanned the negatives. The images were sent back to Earth as electrical signals. The Orbiters took between 200 to 400 photographs each, which covered about 5,562,000 kilometers (3,337,000 miles) of lunar surface.

"Houston, Tranquillity Base here, the Eagle has landed." Six and one half hours later, after sending this message to Mission Control, Neil A. Armstrong and Edwin A. "Buzz" Aldrin stepped onto the surface of the Moon. While on the Moon, the Lunar Module *Eagle* was their home base. It was composed of two sections: the descent stage (which would be left behind on the Moon) and the ascent stage. Both operated together during descent and lunar surface operations. After their investigations, the astronauts lifted off the Moon, using the descent stage as a launching pad.

The Lunar Module on exhibit was built for an unmanned test, but never flew because of the first mission's success. This craft was used instead for ground testing. NASA presented it to the National Air and Space Museum in 1971.

**Rocketry and Space Flight
(Gallery 113)**
From time immemorial, we have wanted to leave the Earth and explore space. Learn about the rockets and engines that enabled us to do it. Trace the development of the concepts of spaceflight from legend and science fiction to reality. The historical artifacts and models exhibited here tell the story of the development of vehicles capable of spaceflight, and highlight some of the major contributions to this field.

As you enter the gallery, you encounter the history of rocket propulsion. The first rockets may have originated in China as early as the 12th or 13th centuries. These were propelled by gunpowder and were probably used as weapons. In the 19th century the Englishman William Congreve designed his rocket system, which transformed larger, more sophisticated black powder rockets into effective weapons. **Congreve rockets** such as this one were used during the War of 1812 and at the battle of Waterloo. At the battle of Fort McHenry in 1814, Francis Scott Key saw the "red glare" of Congreve rockets, which he later described in "The Star Spangled Banner." England and other countries used Congreve rockets until the mid-19th century, although Congreve rockets were often unpredictable.

Englishman William Hale's rocket (developed from the 1840s) eventually replaced the Congreve rocket. Hale eliminated the cumbersome wooden guidesticks, used previously, by designing his rocket to rotate, which somewhat improved its stability and performance.

The British began to use **Hale rockets** during the Crimean War (1853–1856); both Union and Confederate troops used them during the Civil War, although not extensively. More powerful and accurate rifled guns ultimately forced the Hale rocket into retirement in the late 19th century.

From 1920, Robert H. Goddard of Massachusetts developed the first liq-

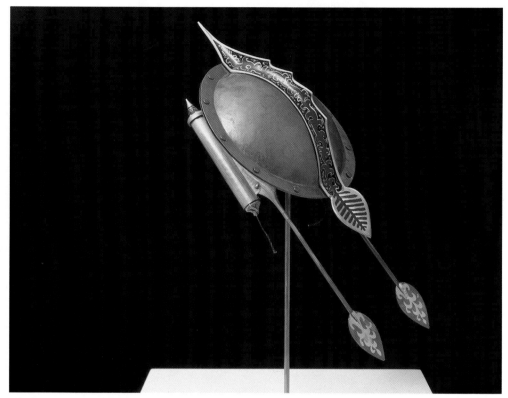

*The first rockets may have originated in China as early as the 12th or 13th centuries. (NASM photo)*

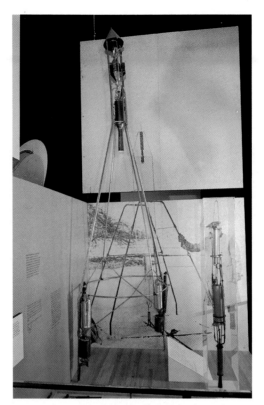

*Extremely modest by today's standards, early Goddard rockets such as this one inspired the development of modern liquid-fuel rockets. (NASM photo)*

uid-fuel rockets, which were potentially more powerful than solid-fuel types. He recognized that they could eventually be used for upper atmospheric and spacecraft exploration. On March 16, 1926, Goddard launched the world's first liquid-fuel rocket; a replica of this rocket is displayed in the Museum's Milestones of Flight gallery. On May 4, 1926, Goddard launched an improved version of the first rocket. The model displayed in this gallery may contain some parts that Goddard used in his March 16, 1926, rocket. Extremely mod-

est by today's standards, these early Goddard rockets may have inspired the development of modern liquid-fuel rockets.

The visitor can trace the history of rocket engine technology through the historic objects on display—from early small liquid propellant powerplants to the modern engines that boost today's spacecraft into orbit.

A cut-away of the **RL-10** engine is here—the first hydrogen/oxygen engine to be flown in space. You can examine the **engine types** used in Chuck

*These upper stage propulsion engines are among the many historical objects in this gallery that contributed to the dream and reality of space flight. (NASM photo)*

*Nineteenth-century French author Jules Verne wrote two novels on space travel; these inspired the first theoreticians of spaceflight. This fanciful projectile chamber is based on the one described in* From the Earth to the Moon, *1865, and* Around the Moon, *1867. (NASM photo)*

Yeager's Bell X-1 and the V-2 rocket. Early **JATO** (Jet-Assisted-Takeoff) engines are on display, including the first U.S. JATO, which was used in 1941. You will also find more exotic engines here, such as the **Orion Nuclear Pulse** and the **Cesium Ion** rocket engines.

Along with the many facts about spaceflight in this gallery, you will also learn about the dream of spaceflight—and the often fantastic forms these dreams took. In the late 19th century, French novelist Jules Verne wrote two books entitled *From the Earth to the Moon*, and *Around the Moon*; these works inspired scientists to take the first steps toward space travel. Verne's heroes, three post-Civil War American artillerists, journey to the Moon in a space capsule that was shot from a cannon. The fanciful craft exhibited to the right of the gallery's entrance was based on Verne's description of his craft. Flying on top of the craft is the American flag, which has as many stars as there were states at the time Verne's books were written.

The flight suits exhibited in this gallery trace the development of the pressurized suit. Requirements for pressurized suits began with deep sea diver's suits like the late-19th-century **Mark V suit** exhibited here; the factors involved in safe ascension from the depths of the sea are similar to those that apply to survival at high altitudes. These early studies resulted in the suits for projects Mercury, Gemini, and Apollo. The Apollo suit is easily recognized by its life-support system, carried as a backpack.

*The pressure suits exhibited here trace the development of the space suit.*
*(NASM photo)*

*Skylab 1 was home in space for three different three-man crews for periods of up to three months. The orbital workshop exhibited here is a backup to the Skylab launched in 1973. (SI no. 79-829)*

## Space Hall (Gallery 114)

Space boosters, guided missiles, and manned spacecraft tower overhead. Here is the history of our explorations in space and the machines that took us there.

The mammoth **Skylab Orbital Workshop, Multiple Docking Adapter**, and **Airlock Module** dominate this gallery. The total Skylab cluster is 36 meters (118 feet) long, and weighs 90,000 kilograms (198,000 pounds). Skylab 1 was home in space for three different three-person crews for periods of up to three months. There the astronauts experimented, ate,

slept, and exercised. The Orbital Workshop, Multiple Docking Adapter, and Airlock Module exhibited here are the flight backups, given to the National Air and Space Museum by NASA in 1975.

One of the highlights of Space Hall is the **Apollo-Soiuz Test Project** (ASTP) exhibit. This rare display shows the full Apollo Command and Service Module docked with the Soviet Soiuz spacecraft by means of an androgenous docking adaptor. This exhibit provides the visitor with the unique opportunity to compare directly the U.S. and Soviet manned spaceflight programs. A product of the

*On July 18, 1975, an Apollo spacecraft and a Soviet Soiuz spacecraft docked in space for the first international manned spaceflight. (SI no. 79-827)*

detente era of the early 1970s, the ASTP was the first international manned spaceflight mission.

In front of the Apollo-Soiuz Test Project is an engineering model of the **Vega** spacecraft currently on loan from the Russian Lavochkin Scientific Production Association. In 1984, the U.S.S.R. launched two spacecraft—**Vega 1** and **Vega 2**—which flew by Venus, depositing scientific devices into the planet's atmosphere, and passed through the tail of Comet Halley, transmitting data

about the comet. Requiring extensive diplomatic, scientific, and technical cooperation, the *Vega* missions marked a new era of international cooperation in the Soviet Space Program. This multinational mission included scientists and technical instruments from nine nations. French scientists designed the main Venus experiment of the *Vega* in which a scientific balloon, a model of which is seen here, was released into the planet's atmosphere to measure cloud activity. While the balloon relayed atmospheric

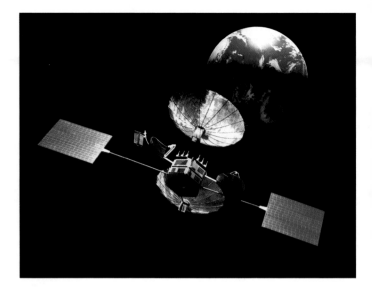

*The TDRS (Tracking and Data Relay Satellite) system determines the exact location of a spacecraft, transmits data, and sends command signals to that spacecraft. (NASA)*

information, a Soviet-designed lander contributed to our knowledge of the planet's surface.

The exhibit "Soviet Solar System Exploration" recounts the history of Soviet missions to the Moon, Venus, and Mars, including both successes and failures since the late 1950s.

NASA designed the wingless **M2-F3 Lifting Body** in an attempt to solve the problems of overheating and vehicle control during return from space. This wingless aircraft derives its aerodynamic lift for flight from its fuselage shape.

The **Tracking and Data Relay Satellite** (TDRS) full-scale model was donated to the National Air and Space Museum by TRW, which designed the original TDRS system for NASA. TDRS 1 through TDRS 6 (with the exception of TDRS 2, which was destroyed when the Space Shuttle *Challenger* exploded) were placed into orbit beginning in 1983. TDRS 7 is planned for launch in 1995. The TDRS system determines the exact location of a spacecraft, transmits data, and sends command signals ordering the spacecraft to perform certain functions.

Learn about expendable launch vehi-cles in an interesting exhibit featuring 1/15-scale models of the Japanese **H-2, Atlas Centaur, Titan-Centaur**, and **Delta rockets**. These are one-time transportation rockets for placing objects in orbit around Earth and launching space probes. Until the advent of the reusable Space Shuttle, the United States depended exclusively on such vehicles. In the future, expendable boosters will complement the Space Shuttle's unique capabilities for working in space.

Here is a 1/15-scale model of the Arianespace's advanced **Ariane 4**. Earlier models of the Ariane rocket have delivered payloads such as telecommunications and weather satellites into orbit. The film and accompanying Ariane 4 models describe to the visitor the European Space Agency's (or ESA's) launch facilities in French Guiana and the many industrial nations involved in the Ariane project.

The imposing German **V-2** of World War II fame was the world's first ballistic missile. Today's intercontinental ballistic liquid-fuel missiles, medium-range missiles, and launch vehicles are direct descendants. The **V-1** flying bomb, suspended from the ceiling, was a German

*The imposing German V-2 of World War II is the grandfather of modern large-scale, liquid-fuel rockets. (NASM photo)*

World War II project, but is an air-breathing pulse-jet, not a rocket. The **Viking 12 Rocket**, an upper atmospheric research or sounding rocket, was designed in 1946 as a vehicle for carrying instruments to altitudes in excess of 305,000 meters (1,000,000 feet). An adjacent cluster of recent rocket-propelled missiles, satellite launch vehicles, and a sounding rocket stand as if poised for

*This Apollo Lunar Module is the backup to the first spacecraft flown in orbit; it is similar to Apollo 11's Eagle. (NASM photo)*

55

*This scene is from the IMAX film* Blue Planet. *Here, looking west over the Sinai Desert and the Red Sea (left) into Egypt, the v-shaped point of the Sinai Peninsula and the nearby Gulf of Aqaba are visible. Giant rifts, clearly seen from space, give clues to the forming of continents. (Copyright Smithsonian Institution/Lockheed Corporation)*

The Dream is Alive, *filmed by the astronauts on a number of Shuttle missions, was released in 1984. In this shot from the film, the Remote Manipulator System arm suspends the giant Long Duration Exposure Facility prior to releasing it into space. (Copyright National Air and Space Museum and Lockheed Corporation)*

*In the IMAX film* To Fly! *the Blue Angels, the U.S. Navy's precision aerobatic team, vividly display the breakthrough of powered flight made possible by 20th-century technology. (NASM photo)*

*The Museum's Zeiss Model VI planetarium instrument, along with other auxiliary audiovisual devices, simulates panoramic views of the heavens and of space travel. (NASM photo)*

flight in a missile pit constructed below floor level.

From the floor of the missile pit, you can get a most unusual view of **Jupiter-C**, the booster that placed America's first satellite, Explorer 1, in orbit. It shares the space with the **Scout** and **Vanguard**, both satellite launchers, and a **Minuteman III** ballistic missile.

The **WAC-Corporal Rocket**, the first American high-altitude sounding rocket, is much smaller than its neighboring giants. Many of the engineers who designed the WAC-Corporal contributed to the **Aerobee** rocket's design. In many respects, the Aerobee, one of the most frequently used sounding rockets of the late 1940s to mid-1980s, was an advanced version of the WAC-Corporal. The rocket on display here is an Aerobee 150. The name "Aerobee" comes from Aerojet (the company that received the contract from the Navy to construct the rocket) and Bumblebee (a series of Navy missile and rocket projects).

Project Vanguard represented the United States's effort to fulfill a commitment made by President Eisenhower in 1955: to place a satellite into orbit as part of its participation in the International Geophysical Year (July 1957 to December 1958). The **Vanguard 1 satellite** was the first successful satellite launched in this series. Former Vanguard project director John P. Hagen donated this back-up Vanguard satellite to the National Air and Space Museum in 1975.

**Langley Theater (Gallery 115)**
Explore our fascination with flight through the air and in space. View Earth from the open cargo bay of the Space Shuttle. Journey to natural and man-made wonders of the world. These and other thrills await you in the National Air and Space Museum's Langley Theater. IMAX® films are projected on the five-story-high screen. Call the Langley Theater for show times (202) 357-1686 or 2700. There is an admission fee.

**Albert Einstein Planetarium (Gallery 201)**
Embark on an astronomical adventure. Learn about the nature of the universe. Realistic astronomical experiences are

This simulated navigational bridge provides an unusual view of jets being catapulted from a carrier flight deck. (NASM photo)

The Boeing F4B-4 was considered to be the finest fighter aircraft of its type during the early 1930s. (SI no. 80-4972)

The Grumman Wildcat F4F fought valiantly in the early days of World War II and established its reputation as a rugged, dependable fighter. (SI no. 80-4973)

produced under the Planetarium's 70-foot (21-meter)-diameter dome, using the West German-made Carl Zeiss Model VI planetarium instrument and hundreds of auxiliary visual effects devices. The Planetarium seats 230 persons; space for a few wheelchairs is also provided. For show times, call (202) 357-1686 or 2700. There is a fee for admission for most programs.

**Sea-Air Operations (Gallery 203)**
Take a moment to familiarize yourself with the history of ship-based flight. Step aboard the simulated aircraft carrier USS *Smithsonian*, CVM-76. Beyond the quarterdeck is the cavernous gray interior of the hangar deck; this is the storage and repair area for the aircraft that take off and land on the flight deck overhead.

The oldest aircraft here is the colorful **Boeing F4B-4**. First ordered in April 1931, the F4B-4 served aboard Navy carriers until 1938, and was considered to be the finest fighter aircraft of its type during the early 1930s.

The **Grumman F4F Wildcat** aircraft fought valiantly at Wake Island in the early days of World War II and established its reputation as a rugged, dependable fighter during the carrier battles of Coral Sea and Midway in 1942. Time after time, the Grumman Wildcat's heavy armament and solid construction enabled it to win air combats against overwhelming odds, and bring its pilots home safely. One of the rarest of war birds is the "Slow but Deadly" **Douglas Dauntless dive bomber**. Ours is an SBD-6 model. In June 1942, at the Battle of Midway, carrier-based Dauntless dive bombers took on a major force of the Imperial Japanese Navy and sank four carriers. These aircraft were exceptionally maneuverable without their bombs, and

*"Slow but Deadly" Douglas Dauntless dive bombers like this one (SBD-6 model) took on a major force of the Imperial Japanese Navy during the Battle of Midway. (SI no. 80-4971)*

*Built continuously from 1954 through 1979, the Douglas A-4C Skyhawk enjoyed the longest production run of any tactical aircraft in history. (SI no. 80-4974)*

aggressive crews exploited this in aerial combat.

Built continuously from 1954 through 1979, the **Douglas A-4 Skyhawk** enjoyed the longest production run of any tactical aircraft in history. Once dubbed "Heinemann's Hot Rod" after designer Ed Heinemann, the lightweight A-4 contrasted sharply with the heavy and expensive aircraft typical of the 1950s. This light attack bomber was capable of carrying an enormous load of weapons, and others like her eventually flew with the Navy's *Blue Angels* flight demonstration team.

Climb up to primary flight control, or Pri-Fly, as it is called. Through its windows you can see and hear a variety of aircraft swooping in over the fantail to an arrested landing below. From the bridge (where catapult operations on the bow can be observed) you go down the ladder, cross the hangar deck and the quarterdeck, and you are back on dry land.

**Don't Miss** new exhibits on World War II carrier warfare in the Pacific and modern carrier aviation.

**World War II Aviation (Gallery 205)**
Roaring directly at the viewer is **Thunder Bird**, a U.S. **Boeing B-17G Flying Fortress** on its way to Wiesbaden, Germany, on August 15, 1944. This tense moment, frozen in time on a giant mural by noted artist Keith Ferris, sets the theme for the gallery: memorializing the men and air machines of World War II.

The combination of speed and firepower made the **Supermarine Spitfire** a deadly machine. The Spitfire's elliptical wing, which reduced drag and increased speed, is its most distinguished characteristic. When the war ended, the Spitfire was the only airplane that had been in continuous production throughout the war—20,351 had rolled off the assembly line. This specimen is a Spitfire Mark VII, a high-altitude version, of which only 140 were produced.

Also on exhibit is the **Mitsubishi A6M5 Zero Model 52**. Well designed,

*The combination of speed and firepower made the Supermarine Spitfire a successful machine. (SI no. 80-2091)*

*Light and maneuverable, the Japanese Mitsubishi A6M5 Zero was a formidable opponent in the hands of a skilled pilot. (NASM photo)*

*For those who flew it, the North American P-51 Mustang was a fighter pilot's airplane and one of the best fighters of World War II. (SI no. 80-2088)*

The Messerschmitt Bf 109 gained its fame during the Battle of Britain and continued its intense rivalry with all Allied aircraft until the close of World War II. (SI no. 80-2090)

The Macchi C.202 was one of Italy's most advanced World War II fighters. (SI no. 80-2089).

light, and maneuverable, the Japanese Zero was a formidable opponent in the hands of a skilled pilot. Against later, more-powerful American fighters, however, the Zero lost ground and became an easy target by the end of the war.

For those who flew it, the **North American P-51 Mustang** was a fighter pilot's airplane and one of the best fighters of World War II. Unlike other well-known and widely used fighters of that time, the P-51 was first conceived during the war and built on the basis of combat experience. The markings on the Museum's P-51D (the yellow and black checkerboard design on the nose, and

the letters "Willit Run?") are patterned after a P-51D flown in Britain by the 351st Fighter Squadron, 353d Fighter Group, 8th Air Force.

The Mustang's frequent opponent was the **Messerschmitt Bf 109**, combat-proven in the Spanish Civil War. Produced in the largest quantity of any Axis aircraft, the Messerschmitt existed in a number of designs. Ours is the Bf 109G Gustav used later in World War II. This aircraft gained its fame as the major opponent of the Spitfire. It continued its intense rivalry with all Allied aircraft until the close of World War II.

The **Macchi C.202** was one of Italy's

most advanced World War II fighters. Outside Italy, however, it failed to achieve as much fame as contemporary fighters of other nations. Known as the Folgore, meaning "lightning," the pilots who flew it lauded its fingerlight handling and its superb agility. The Macchi C.202 is one of two remaining aircraft of this type anywhere in the world. Its early history is obscure, but it was one of many enemy World War II aircraft the Army brought to the United States for evaluation and testing after the war.

The **Martin B-26B Marauder "Flak Bait"** (nose only here) flew more missions over Europe than any other Allied airplane of World War II. With 202 operational sorties to its credit, this medium bomber had the longest and most colorful combat history of any aircraft in the Museum. Despite their initially high rate of accidents in training, the Marauders soon vindicated themselves with the greatest bombing accuracy and lowest loss rate of any American aircraft.

"Flak Bait" was given its name after "Flea Bait," a nickname for the dog belonging to the aircraft's pilot. The original paint is still bright, but more than a thousand patched flak holes bear witness to the fact that this most famous of Marauders was indeed appropriately named.

*In contrast to many of its contemporaries in the Allied air services, the SPAD XIII had an enviable reputation of strength and durability under the most demanding combat maneuvers. (NASM photo)*

### Legend, Memory, and the Great War in the Air (Gallery 206)

This exhibit places aircraft and air power in proper perspective and examines the contradictions between the myths and realities of World War I combat. The aircraft exhibited here took to the skies during the Great War in the air—World War I.

The **Fokker D.VII** is considered by most historians to be Germany's best fighter in that war, rightfully feared by its opponents. It reached front-line squadrons early in May 1918, too late to turn the tide of battle. This Fokker D.VII landed by mistake on a forward aerodrome behind the front lines on November 9, 1918, two days before the Armistice. The "U-10" markings represent the pilot's former affiliation with the 10th Uhlan cavalry regiment.

Rugged and fast, the French SPAD airplanes fought well in the hands of experienced pilots. On exhibit is a **SPAD XIII**, one of three examples left in existence (8,472 were originally built). This aircraft was a refinement of the SPAD VII, with twin machine guns and a more powerful engine. This SPAD XIII is the most thoroughly documented and complete U.S. World War I fighter in any collection.

Also on exhibit in this gallery is a **Sopwith Snipe**, a development of the famous Sopwith Camel. Historians remember the Snipe as the first standard postwar Royal Air Force fighter; its wartime career was limited to service with only three squadrons. Major W. G. Barker made the Snipe famous by single-handedly battling 15 enemy fighters. Barker later received the Victoria Cross from King George V for his bravery.

The **Voisin VIII** bomber was a strong and serviceable type based on a pre-war design. It was built beginning in 1916, in an attempt to equip the French Air Service with a faster and more powerful aircraft capable of carrying a substantial bomb load deep into Germany's industrial region. The poor handling qualities and the disappointing performance of the 200 h.p. Peugeot engine, however, forced the French to use it on night missions to avoid fighter opposition. This Voisin was transferred to the Smithsonian Institution in 1918.

The Germans and other Central Powers used the Albatros more than any

In all, more than 1,000 Voisin VIIIs were manufactured, including a small number of ground attack versions. Twenty-six French squadrons were equipped with these aircraft, as well as most of the Allied Air Services, who used them throughout the war. (NASM photo)

The Albatros was the fighter most widely used by the Germans and other Central Powers during World War I. NASM's Albatros is the D. Va type. (NASM photo)

other aircraft during World War I. The aircraft exhibited in this gallery, standing resplendent with "circus" tail markings of *Jagdstaffel* 46, is an **Albatros D. Va** type. It was in this type, not the Fokker DR.I Triplane, that Baron Manfred von Richtofen (the "Red Baron") scored 59 of his 80 victories. The origin of the word "Stropp" is unknown, but is typical of individualized markings created by the German pilots. This Albatros fought on the Western Front, was damaged in battle, and was captured. It is one of the two remaining examples in existence.

*Exploring the Planets gallery highlights the history and achievements of planetary explorations, both Earth-based and by spacecraft. (NASM photo)*

## Exploring the Planets (Gallery 207)

How long have we gazed at distant planets suspended in the night sky? As long as anyone can remember. What have our observations revealed? This exhibit highlights the history and achievements of planetary explorations, both Earth-based and by spacecraft.

As you enter the gallery, stop at the exhibit called "Tools of Planetary Exploration." Here, you will learn about the Surveyor spacecraft, five of which landed on the Moon between June 2, 1966, and January 10, 1968. Each Surveyor photographed the lunar surface and measured its mechanical, electrical, and thermal properties. The last three missions also analyzed the chemical composition of the surface materials. On exhibit in this case is the **Surveyor 3 television camera**, which landed on the Moon as part of Surveyor 3 on April 20, 1967. On November 24, 1969, the crew of Apollo 12 carried the camera back to Earth. This photo shows Apollo 12 astronaut Alan Bean grasping the Surveyor 3 camera with his right hand. The Apollo 12 Lunar Module is on the horizon, about 100 meters (330 feet) away.

Early space probes, launched more than two decades ago, were the first to encounter the asteroid belt and the first to fly past the more-distant planets such as Jupiter and Saturn.

Mars, the Red Planet, goal of space expeditions detailed in science fiction, has begun to yield its secrets to unmanned spacecraft. The first flyby missions—Mariner 4 (1964) and Mariners 6 and 7 (1969)—looked down on a lifeless, cratered surface reminiscent of the Moon. Mariner 9 arrived at Mars during

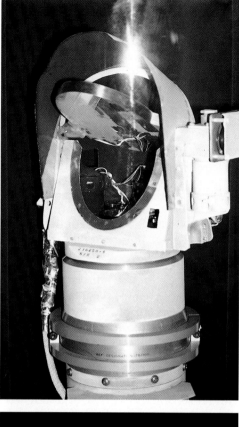

*Above: This Surveyor television camera landed on the Moon as part of Surveyor 3 on April 20, 1967. (NASM photo)* **Bottom photo**: *Apollo 12 astronaut Alan Bean grasps the front of the Surveyor 3 camera; the Lunar Module is behind him on the horizon. (NASM photo)*

a major dust storm; it began orbiting Mars on November 13, 1971, but was unable to transmit images until February 6, 1972. When the storms cleared, scientists on Earth saw a dramatically different view of Mars. In contrast to the cratered Moon-like surface of the southern hemisphere observed by earlier Mariners, the northern hemisphere was a region of volcanoes, lava fields, canyons, and eroded valleys. Mariner 9 tumbled out of control on October 27, 1972, when its supply of attitude control fuel was exhausted.

Two **Viking** spacecraft, each vehicle consisting of two parts, sped toward Mars in 1975. The Orbiter section stayed above the planet for its observations; the Lander section descended, and touched down on the surface. Aside from their transmissions of breathtaking images of the planet, the two Viking spacecraft confirmed the existence of storms of reddish dust that had been seen from Earth by powerful telescopes. The spacecrafts' instruments measured Martian weather and analyzed the Martian chemistry. Viking 1 now belongs to the National Air and Space Museum; a plaque renaming the spacecraft the Thomas A. Mutch Memorial Station is on display in gallery 100, and will be attached to the Lander when astronauts journey to Mars and set foot on Chryse Planitia, the landing site.

The full-scale engineering test model of the **Voyager** spacecraft displayed here approximates two sent to explore Jupiter, Saturn, Uranus, and Neptune. Launched on different trajectories, they passed Jupiter during March and July 1979, and cruised on toward Saturn, Voyager 2 several months behind Voyager 1. The images of Jupiter they sent back revealed to scientists that Jupiter has rings and that Io, one of Jupiter's moons, has at least seven active volcanoes.

Voyager 1's encounter with Saturn occurred during the summer of 1980, with Voyager 2 following nine months later. As Voyager 1 approached Saturn, the spacecraft detected increasingly more detail about the planet's rings. Once thought to be discretely separate bands of material, scientists now know Saturn's rings to consist of thousands of small bands that differ in particle size and composition. After its exploration of Saturn, Voyager 1 proceeded on a path taking it directly out of the solar system, while Voyager 2 began a five-year journey to dark-ringed Uranus, which it encountered in January 1986. During the summer of 1989, Voyager 2 reached Neptune, and provided the first close-up observations of the planet and its moons.

**Don't Miss** the exhibit called "Exploring Comets," which traces the study of comets from the earliest historical observation to the international Halley's Comet Watch. Families will enjoy the Family of the Sun display, consisting of children's art and an accompanying audio tape.

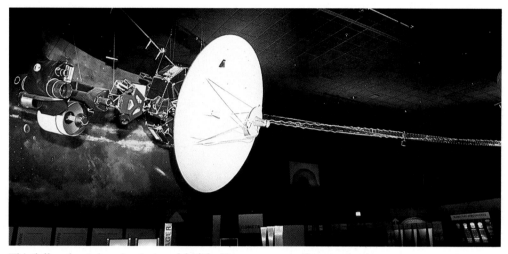

*This full-scale engineering test model of the Voyager spacecraft approximates two sent to explore Jupiter, Saturn, Uranus, and Neptune. (SI no. 80-13717)*

*In this Wright brothers EX biplane, the* Vin Fiz *adventurer Cal Rogers attempted to make a transcontinental flight in 30 days or less. (SI 80-2081)*

*The Douglas World Cruiser* Chicago *was one of the two aircraft to make the first flight around the world. (NASM photo)*

*Five years after Charles Lindbergh's historic flight, Amelia Earhart flew this red Lockheed Vega solo across the Atlantic, becoming the first woman to do so. (SI no. 80-2082)*

## Pioneers of Flight (Gallery 208)

Since the Wright brothers flew at Kitty Hawk, men and women have had to break both physical and psychological barriers to flight. In these historic aircraft, individuals strived to claim their place in aviation history.

In 1911, William Randolph Hearst offered a prize of $50,000 to the first pilot to make a transcontinental flight in fewer than 30 days. After 20 hours of flying lessons, adventurer Cal Rogers acquired a **Wright EX biplane** and a sponsor (the Armour Company) and prepared to depart for California. The airplane was decorated with the trademark of an Armour soft-drink product, "Vin Fiz." In addition to the prize money, Rogers was to receive five dollars from Armour for every mile he flew. But it was not until almost two months later, after 70 landings, a number of which were crashes, and extensive repairs to the aircraft, that Rogers reached his destination.

In May 1923, this **Fokker T-2** became the first aircraft to fly nonstop coast to coast. The flight took 26 hours and 50 minutes.

The **Douglas World Cruiser "Chicago"** was one of two aircraft to make the first flight around the world. In addition to the prototype, the Army built four of these Douglas airplanes for this specific purpose. Only the *Chicago* and the *New Orleans* were destined to survive the effort.

The design of Amelia Earhart's red **Lockheed Vega** is related to that of the Northrop Alpha in gallery 102. Both were designed by Jack Northrop, and have the same streamlined shape. Exactly five years after Lindbergh's historic solo flight across the Atlantic in May 1932, Amelia Earhart flew this Vega solo across the Atlantic, becoming the first woman to do so.

*The Lindberghs flew the Lockheed Sirius* Tingmissartoq *to the Orient by way of the "great circle route." (SI no. 80-2092)*

In 1931, Charles and Anne Morrow Lindbergh flew to the Orient in this **Lockheed Sirius**—the first aircraft to reach the Far East by way of the "great circle route." Lindbergh described their trip as a vacation, with "no start or finish, no diplomatic or commercial significance, and no records to be sought." In 1933, while Lindbergh was technical advisor for Pan American Airways, the Lindberghs used the same Sirius to cross the Atlantic, researching flight paths for Pan American Airways. In Godthaab, Greenland, an Eskimo boy named the aircraft *Tingmissartoq*, meaning "one who flies like a bird." The aircraft bears this name, painted on the side by the same Eskimo boy.

The **Gossamer Condor** successfully demonstrated sustained, maneuverable human-powered flight on August 23, 1977, winning the coveted $95,000 Kremer Prize that British industrialist Henry Kremer established in 1959. Dr. Paul MacCready and Dr. Peter Lissamen designed the Condor, which is constructed of thin aluminum tubes and mylar plastic, supported with stainless steel wire. Championship bicyclist and hang-glider enthusiast Bryan Allen flew the Condor for 7 minutes, 2.7 seconds, over a closed course to earn the prize.

**Where Next, Columbus? (Gallery 209)**
Five hundred years ago, Christopher Columbus sailed west across the Atlantic, using the stars to guide him. Today, modern explorers are charting a course that may eventually take humanity out among the stars themselves. How and why have we come from seafaring to spacefaring? What challenges and choices do we face now?

The newest permanent exhibition at the National Air and Space Museum, *Where Next, Columbus?* asks visitors to consider the motives and methods of exploration, as well as the options and possibilities for further space exploration.

The first section of the exhibition, "Exploring This World," is a walk through

*On August 23, 1977, Bryan Allen and the Gossamer Condor successfully demonstrated sustained, maneuverable manpowered flight. (NASM photo)*

*Entrance to* Where Next, Columbus?
*(NASM photo: C. Russo)*

the past 500 years of exploration. Three case studies in exploration—Spain's Enterprise of the Indies, the young United States' Corps of Discovery to the West, and the Cold War era American mission to the Moon—are shown on one side of the entryway. These examples illuminate the motives, technologies, risks, costs, and results of exploration. On the opposite side, the changing conception of this world as revealed through key maps of the past 500 years, as well as our changing conception of the universe as revealed through cosmographical diagrams and astronomical images, is shown. Today neither this world nor the universe at large bears much resemblance to the concepts of 500 years ago. Exploration—by traveling to places and by observing them from a distance—has had tremendous impact.

"Challenges for Space Explorers" is a bridge between the past and future. In a setting that suggests a spaceship, visitors consider physiological effects of weightlessness such as muscle atrophy and bone calcium loss, the radiation risk to space travelers, and options for faster or more efficient space transportation systems.

The focus of this area is an interactive video program that asks the question, "Why explore?" Visitors consider a variety of opinions—positive and negative—about motives for exploration today.

"Exploring New Worlds in Space," the exhibition's next section, is a 3,000-square-foot simulated Martian landscape. Visitors follow paths in a valley on Mars; steep canyon walls rise to the ceiling on two sides, and a vista across the valley opens in murals on two walls. Visitors may follow either or both paths

*In the "Exploring This World" section visitors are invited to look back at the history of exploration—motives, methods and consequences—from the time of Columbus's arrival in the New World (1492) to the Apollo moon landing in 1969. (NASM photo: C. Russo)*

through the Mars site. The theme of one path is robotic exploration, and of the other, human.

Highlights along the robotic path include a half-scale model of the Mars Observer spacecraft launched in September, 1992, with related up-to-date weather reports from Mars; a full-scale model of the Russian Mars rover, scheduled for launch in 1996; and an experimental microbot explorer ("Genghis") from the MIT artificial intelligence laboratory. An interactive video allows visitors to plot a robotic mission to Mars.

Highlights along the path of human exploration include a video of explorers at work in other worlds under the sea, in Antarctica, and on the Moon; an advanced spacesuit designed for planetary exploration; a habitat nestled into a hillside, showing some of the requirements for sustaining human life in a distant world; and a thriving hydroponic salad garden. The human path culminates in another custom-designed Mars mission simulation. As in the robotic mission, the visitor plays the lead role in making decisions about mission objectives and landing sites. This time, however, the visitor interacts with a crew and focuses on the human life support aspects of space exploration, monitoring crew health and life support systems and responding to an emergency en route to Mars.

This area concludes with a display about the environmental ethics of exploring new worlds, and particularly the concept of altering other environments (terraforming) to make them more habitable.

As visitors leave the Mars site, they may enter a small theater to view three short films produced for the exhibition:

*In the section "Challenges for Space Explorers," visitors enter a hypothetical spacecraft to confront the physical challenges of space travel, such as radiation, microgravity, high-speed collisions with meteoroids and inefficient transportation. (NASM photo: C. Russo)*

*A 3,000 square-foot simulated Martian landscape—complete with an advanced spacesuit designed for planetary exploration and a model of a Russian Mars Rover—is one of the highlights of* Where Next, Columbus? *The section also includes a half-scale model of the Mars Observer, launched in 1992 on a three-year mission. (NASM photo: C. Russo)*

a computer-animated tour of our solar system in "Otherworlds"; a claymation Albert Einstein, using movie clips to separate science fiction from science fact, in "Spacefaring"; and movie encounters with aliens, exploring stereotypes that reveal some assumptions we make about ourselves and others in "Contact!"

The third and final section, "To the Stars," shifts our scale of distance and time from the solar system to the galaxy. At the entrance to this area, a uniquely accurate mural of the Milky Way leads into a room-sized model of our neighborhood in the galaxy: a three-dimensional stellarium shows the locations and magnitude of more than 700 stars within 50 light years of the Sun. The stellarium prompts visitors to realize how much more vast the distances are between stars than planets, how much more challenging the prospects are for interstellar travel compared to planetary travel, and how we may explore by means other than travel.

Highlights of the "Stars" portion of the gallery include a display tracing the history of scientists' efforts to "listen" with powerful radio telescopes for signs

*"Exploring New Worlds" section of the exhibition. (NASM photo: C. Russo)*

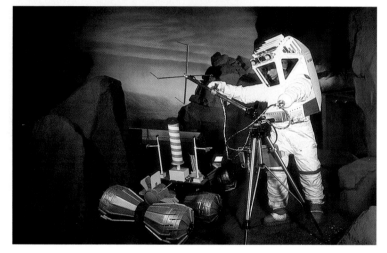

*This detail of an advanced spacesuit designed for planetary exploration and a model of a Russian Mars Rover are on display in the "Exploring New Worlds" section. (NASM photo: C. Russo)*

of life elsewhere in the universe, and an interactive computer video for estimating the probability that other civilizations exist in the galaxy.

Before exiting the gallery, visitors may pause at a public opinion poll to consider some questions about future exploration.

**Don't Miss**: The portal at the entrance to the gallery frames an image of our planet as seen from space. This is an image of cloudless Earth, assembled pixel by pixel from years of satellite data by a team that includes a scientist, an artist, and a high-speed computer.

*Astronaut Alan Shepard, the first U.S. citizen in space, traveled there in 1961 aboard this one-man Mercury* Freedom *7. (SI no. 79-757)*

## Apollo to the Moon (Gallery 210)

The technology of spaceflight developed rapidly in both the United States and Soviet Union. Fewer than 10 years after the first manned spaceflight, men were actually walking on the Moon's surface. This gallery traces the development of manned spaceflight from its roots in early rocketry to the success of the Apollo lunar program and the Skylab space station.

The Soviets launched the world's first artificial satellite, Sputnik 1, on October 4, 1957. The United States's first program to launch a satellite was Project Vanguard. On December 6, 1957, our attempt to launch a **Vanguard satellite** met with spectacular failure; the remains of the actual satellite, recovered after the explosion, are exhibited in the hands of the figure of Uncle Sam at the gallery's entrance. From that first failed launch to our landing on the Moon, "Uncle Sam" has maintained the steady effort that has yielded the objects and events shown in this gallery.

The huge **Saturn F-1** engine, which provided propulsion for the first stage of the Saturn V rocket, is 5.6 meters (18 feet, 4 inches) long. The 111-meter (363-foot)-tall Saturn V rocket was the largest rocket in the world at the time of its de-

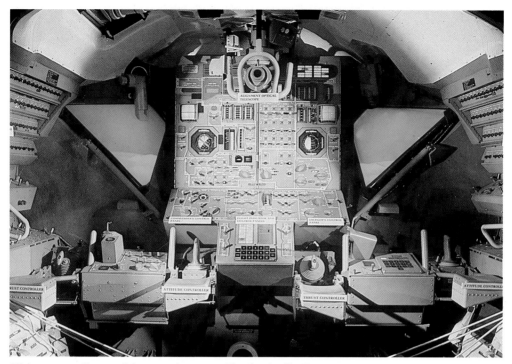

*Visitors get a glimpse of the controls operated by the Apollo 17 astronauts during their mission to and from the Moon. (SI no. 79-765)*

velopment in the early 1960s, and the F-1 engine was the most powerful rocket engine at that time.

Soviet cosmonaut Yuri A. Gagarin became the first man to orbit the earth on April 12, 1961. Twenty-three days later, astronaut Alan B. Shepard made the first U.S. manned space flight in "**Freedom 7**" on May 5, 1961. *Freedom 7* soared to an altitude of 186 kilometers (116 miles). Although Shepard's flight lasted only 15 minutes, the *Freedom 7* mission was the first step to the Moon. It gave President Kennedy the confidence 20 days later to make his speech about putting a man on the Moon. You can see a videotape of the speech near the spacecraft.

Nearby is a full-size mock-up of the interior of a **Lunar Module** identical in appearance to the cockpits of those that landed on the Moon. On an actual mission, the two astronauts traveling in the lunar module stood before the windows as they controlled the craft during both descent to and ascent from the lunar surface. Look through the cockpit windows and you will see the landing of the Apollo 17 Lunar Module *Challenger*, as seen by Eugene A. Cernan and Harrison H. "Jack" Schmitt.

An exhibit entitled "Astronaut Tools

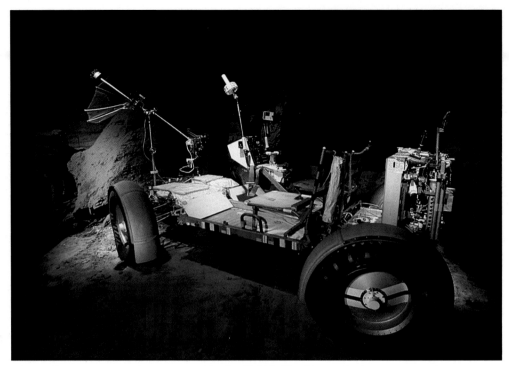

*The Apollo 17 astronauts drove a Lunar Roving Vehicle like this one during their December 1972 mission. (SI no. 79-832)*

and Equipment" contains the navigation aids and personal equipment used on a variety of missions. Visitors can see the space suit that John Glenn wore on February 20, 1962, when he became the first U.S. citizen to orbit the earth.

The Space Food exhibit illustrates the improvements in technology that have made eating in space much more like eating on Earth. In 1962, John Glenn ate pureed food out of toothpaste tubes; later, in 1985, a Space Shuttle crew drank Coke and Pepsi out of specially designed cans.

An exhibit case nearby highlights Apollo 11 and Apollo 17—the first and last Apollo missions to the Moon. The first manned exploration of the Moon occurred July 20 through 21, 1969. Astronauts Neil A. Armstrong and Edwin E. "Buzz" Aldrin explored the surface for 2 hours and 15 minutes. During this time, they deployed two experiments as part of the Early Apollo Scientific Experiment Package, and collected 21 kilograms (46 pounds) of lunar samples for return to Earth. The suits worn by Armstrong and Aldrin are on exhibit in this case. The visitor will see that the Apollo 17 astronauts performed more complicated experiments, using more advanced equipment. Apollo 17, the last manned exploration of the Moon during the Apollo program, occurred December 12 through 15, 1972. Astronauts Eugene Cernan and Harrison Schmitt performed three separate Extravehicular Activities (EVAs), totaling a record 22 hours and 6 minutes, and collected 112 kilograms (247 pounds) of material for return to Earth. They also drove a **Lunar Roving Vehicle** similar to the one on display. You can see that Eugene Cernan's Apollo 17 space suit is a more advanced version of the type worn by Armstrong and Aldrin.

In December 1965, the two-person **Gemini 7** carried astronauts Frank Borman and James Lovell, Jr., into orbit; 11 days later, Gemini 6, with Walter Schirra and Thomas Stafford aboard, performed a rendezvous with Gemini 7. The 14-day Gemini 7 mission was significant in two respects. First, it proved that man could physically withstand weightlessness for the length of time required on a lunar mission. Second, the mission's rendezvous, the first ever conducted, proved the feasibility of a critical element of a lunar landing mission: the ability to meet and dock in space.

The **Skylab 4 Command Module** was used to ferry astronauts Gerald P. Carr, Edward G. Gibson, and William R. Pogue to the Skylab Orbital Workshop. (Behind you in gallery 114 is the backup Skylab Orbital Workshop.) Skylab 4 was the longest U.S. space mission to date. The crew lived in the Skylab Orbital Workshop for 84 days, demonstrating that humans can live and work in space for long periods of time.

**Don't Miss** the Astronaut Survival Equipment, including a sea water drinking kit and shark repellant. Also of interest is a film entitled *25 Years of Space Exploration*, which consists of five-minute segments of some memorable events related to spaceflight, politics, the arts, and entertainment.

### Flight and the Arts (Gallery 211)

This gallery is designed to be an exhibit space for temporary art exhibitions thematically related to air and space flight. Some of these shows explore, through art and culture, the meaning of developments in astronomy, ballooning, aviation, and space flight. Others, in turn, explore the effects that those developments have had on art and culture. The Museum's art collection is subject matter based, and ranges from early ballooning through the present.

The Art Department strives to keep the Museum's art exhibits as dynamic as their subjects, encouraging artists to continue to introduce new perceptions of air and space flight.

### Beyond the Limits: Flight Enters the Computer Age (Gallery 213)

If there has been one development that has most affected flight technology since the opening of the Museum in 1976, it has been the application of the digital computer to flight. That phenomenon is the subject of the Beyond the Limits gallery.

Designing, building, and flying aircraft have always been activities that require calculations and data collecting. In the 1930s, aeronautical labs and companies employed dozens of "computers"—people whose job it was to digest and analyze large quantities of wind tunnel data, using pencil and paper, and perhaps a mechanical desk calculator. Meanwhile, in the cockpit, pilots carried in their pockets "flight computers"—specialized slide rules that helped them navigate over long distances.

By the end of the 1940s, the word

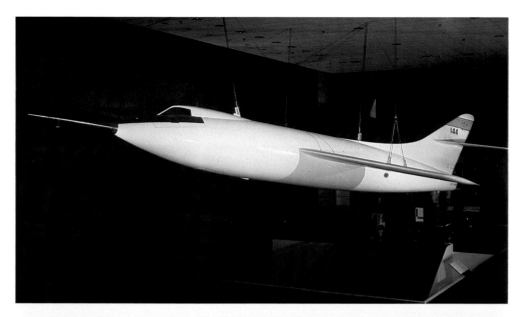

*Above*: On November 20, 1953, A. Scott Crossfield became the first pilot to fly twice the speed of sound (Mach 2) in this rocket-propelled Douglas D-558-2 Skyrocket. (SI no. 79-762) **Bottom photo**: Nicknamed "the missile with a man in it," the sleek Lockheed F-104 Starfighter was the first interceptor in our nation's service to be able to fly at sustained speeds at twice the speed of sound. (SI no. 79-760)

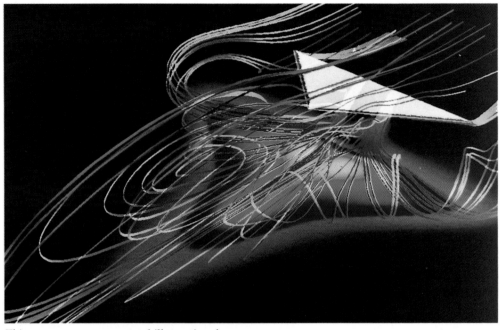

*This supercomputer-generated illustration shows the flow of air over an airfoil as it lifts off. (NASA photo)*

computer meant a machine that could do those calculations. The first computers, built with vacuum tubes, were heavy, expensive, and unreliable. Nonetheless aerospace companies were among the first to purchase and use these machines. Despite the limits of these machines, aerospace engineers felt that designing new-generation jet-powered planes and rockets demanded them. Computers were crucial in getting these craft off the drawing board but were much too bulky to be carried on board.

All that changed in the late 1950s, with the invention of the integrated circuit, familiar to us all today as the silicon "chip." A single chip could replace racks of fragile and heavy tubes. Now it was possible to bring computing power into the air as well as to use it on the ground. The first application of chips

*NASA's radical X-29 aircraft, built by the Grumman Corporation, features wings that sweep forward. The X-29 is extremely maneuverable, and would be too unstable to fly without several on-board control computers. (NASM photo)*

was in the guidance system for the Minuteman ballistic missile. It was followed shortly by the on-board guidance and control computer for the Apollo spacecraft that took men to the Moon.

With Minuteman and Apollo as pioneers, chips became faster, more rugged, and cheaper. Today, consumers can buy a pocket computer far more powerful than the ones that took men to the Moon in 1969.

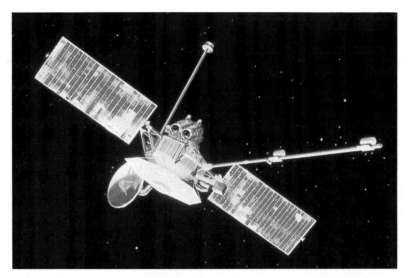

*Mariner 10 was NASA's first dual planet mission and the first mission designed to explore Mercury. Built by the Boeing Company under the direction of NASA's Jet Propulsion Laboratory, the spacecraft carried an on-board computer that enabled Earth-based engineers to program its trajectory through space. (NASA photo)*

For the aerospace community, the computer is a tool, no more and no less. The gallery focuses not on the computers themselves but on the aerospace applications of computers, illustrating how these have transformed the everyday jobs of pilots, engineers, astronauts, and scientists. In the past, the airplane or spacecraft designer relied on calculating instruments to help him create light, safe, and fast machines. Although the basics have not changed, **Computer-Aided-Design/Computer-Assisted-Manufacture** (CAD/CAM) has transformed the design process in recent years. Air traffic controllers and navigators also depend on computer technology every day. The visitor can manipulate work stations to experience these computer uses.

*Unlike most computers, which use printed circuit boards, the CRAY-1 supercomputer is laboriously wired by hand. Connecting the various circuits of the machine by short, hand-soldered wires allows electrical signals to carry data from one part of the machine to another more quickly. The computer's circular shape also lessens the distance—and time—for signals to travel.*

*Above*: *An important project in pioneering technology for future military aircraft is the HiMAT (Highly Maneuverable Aircraft Technology program), which incorporates advanced design features for far greater maneuverability. (NASA)* **Bottom photo**: *An unconventional machine with a swept forward wing, the Grumman X-29's advanced flight control computer creates artificial stability in an airplane designed to be unstable. (NASA)*

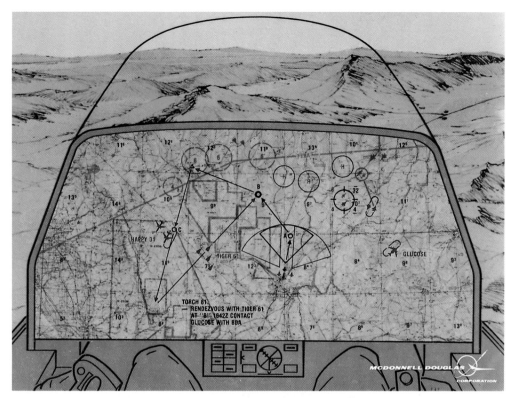

*This computer-enhanced cockpit, used to train pilots and astronauts, illustrates the vital role computers play in aerospace technology every day. (NASM photo)*

See two experimental NASA aircraft—the **HiMAT**, and a full-scale model of the **Grumman X-29**. The HiMAT (Highly Maneuverable Aircraft Technology) is an important project in pioneering technology for future military aircraft. It incorporates a number of advanced design features for far greater maneuverability than is currently attainable.

An unconventional machine with a swept-forward wing, the X-29 was deliberately designed to be unstable in order to enhance the aircraft's maneuver-ability. As a result, no human pilot can respond quickly enough to maintain control of the airplane during maneuvers. An advanced flight control computer is used to create artificial stability through small control inputs.

Other interesting exhibits, such as a full-size Space Shuttle cockpit simulator and a theater devoted to the use of computers for training pilots and astronauts, illustrate the vital role computers play in aerospace technology every day.

*The Garber Facility's highly trained staff handles a variety of restoration projects, from fabric work to rebuilding engines. (NASM photo)*

*This is the display/storage area at the Paul E. Garber Preservation, Restoration, and Storage Facility in Suitland, Maryland. (NASM photo)*

# PAUL E. GARBER PRESERVATION, RESTORATION, AND STORAGE FACILITY

In 1980, the National Air and Space Museum renamed its Silver Hill restoration facility to honor the man who contributed greatly to the formation of the Museum, Paul E. Garber (1899–1992). Here the Museum preserves and stores aircraft, spacecraft, and other artifacts, and restores battered aircraft to represent a specific period in their history.

Although the facility has been used since the mid-1950s as a preservation, restoration, and storage center, some of the buildings were opened to the public in 1977 as a "no-frills" museum. These areas are open for regularly scheduled tours. Visitors see approximately 90 aircraft as well as spacecraft, engines, propellers, models, and other flight-related objects. Guides conduct tours that include a behind-the-scenes look at the workshop where all phases of the restoration process are handled—from fabric work to rebuilding engines.

The restoration staff work on several projects at any one time. The Garber Facility's staff has completed restoration on 67 artifacts since 1959.

It takes anywhere from 2,000 to 30,000 work hours to return an aircraft or spacecraft to its original condition (2,000 for the Wright Flyer, and 18,000 for the Arado 234), and it requires highly specialized skills. The Garber staff carefully documents each restoration project with photography and data corresponding to each step of the process. Procedures like this have been described, along with historical background material, in a series of Museum publications, *Famous Aircraft of the National Air and Space Museum.*

Free tours of the Garber Facility are available Monday through Friday at 10 a.m.; Saturday and Sunday at 10 a.m. and 1 p.m. Reservations must be made at least two weeks in advance. Call (202) 357-1440 or write: Tour Scheduler, Office of Volunteer Services, National Air and Space Museum, Washington, D.C. 20560.

Individuals or groups will be accepted for the guided tours, which last between two and three hours. Special tours for handicapped visitors are available upon request. Note: there is no heating or air conditioning in the display/storage areas, so visitors are advised to dress appropriately.

# DEPARTMENTS AND RESEARCH FACILITIES

The National Air and Space Museum brings to its visitors the story of discovery and invention in aviation and space technology, and of the resulting applications that have changed all of our lives. The aim is to explore and portray the history and the science of aeronautics and spaceflight.

The Museum is a living entity, undergoing constant change to keep its exhibits and programs up to date. There are five research departments: Aeronautics, Space History, the Center for Earth and Planetary Studies, the Laboratory for Astrophysics, and the Art department. Their staff members help organize exhibitions, maintain the collections, and contribute to a variety of public programs and scholarly symposia. Curators augment and review the collections, conduct research, and develop the content of future exhibits.

The Museum offers the following visiting fellowships for scholars and students: the Daniel and Florence Guggenheim Fellowship; the Alfred V. Verville Fellowship; the Charles A. Lindbergh Chair; the Martin Marietta Chair in Space History; and the International Fellowship. The Museum also offers internships to undergraduate and graduate students.

The Education Division provides interpretive programs to enhance visitors' understanding of the science, history, and technology represented by the Museum's collection of original aerospace artifacts. Its staff members serve as liaisons between the curatorial departments and the visitors, reaching out to teachers, school children, community organizations, individuals with special

*The Admiral DeWitt Clinton Ramsey Room houses the rare aeronautica and astronautica of the National Air and Space Museum Library. (NASM photo)*

needs, and the general public.

The Education Division also provides daily science demonstrations and public tours for walk-in visitors. In addition, prearranged docent-led tours and science demonstrations are offered on such topics as aviation history, planetary science, Earth science, and space exploration. All tours can accommodate visitors with special needs.

The National Air and Space Museum Library, with 30,000 books and 11,000 bound journal volumes, is a repository for the history of aviation, aeronautics and astronautics, Earth and planetary studies, and astronomy and astrophysics. A collection of rare materials is housed in the library's Ramsey Room. Library staff members offer reference services to visiting researchers. The li-

*The Archival Analog Videodisc system has proved to be an effective medium for storing 100,000 black-and-white and color photographs on each disc, and indexing them. The researcher is selecting a photo from the videodisc and making a paper copy for reference. (NASM photo)*

brary is open to the public from 10:00 a.m. to 4:00 p.m., Monday through Friday, by appointment.

The National Air and Space Museum Archives is responsible for document, film, and photograph collections relating to the history and technology of aviation and aerospace. The Archives is divided into two units. The ready reference materials, vertical files, frequently used photograph collections, and archives administration are located in Room 3100 at the Museum in Washington, D.C. The second unit is located in Building 12 at the Paul E. Garber Facility for Preservation, Restoration, and Storage, in Suitland, Maryland. The Archives at the Garber Facility houses the main body of the document collections including more than two million aircraft engineering drawings from the 1890s to the 1970s, either on microfilm or in paper format.

The archival collection contains approximately 10,000 cubic feet of material including an estimated 1.5 million photographs, 700,000 feet of motion picture film, and 2 million technical drawings. The Archives is open to the public by appointment. Inquiries by letter are also welcome.

The Archives has reproduced many of its photographic images on analogue videodiscs. Each videodisc contains approximately 100,000 images (except for videodisc 4, which contains 50,000). Discs 1 and 2 cover various air and space subjects; discs 3 and 4 reproduce the U.S. Air Force pre-1954 photo collection; discs 5 and 6 reproduce a set of the NASA public release collection, including lunar missions from Ranger 7 through Apollo 17 and Space Shuttle missions STS-1 through STS-61C. These discs are available for sale.

The Museum has an active publications program. Scientific and historical books, exhibition catalogs, monographs on single aircraft, and proceedings of symposia on various air and space topics are among the titles published. For a publications brochure, write to the Office of Publications, National Air and Space Museum, Washington, D.C., 20560.